Penny's Puppies

By Penny Spade

ISBN: 9798328956673

DEDICATION

This book is dedicated to my five grandchildren: Tyler, Camden, Gemma, Thomas and Andrew.

This book is for them.

CONTENTS

INTRODUCTION

This book is about my journey from growing up in a small town in Texas to moving to California, becoming a mom, working in the corporate world for many years and ending up becoming a puppy rescuer in Cabo San Lucas, Mexico. Many people have animals that have changed their lives in one way or another. Becoming a foster mom to vulnerable, innocent puppies when no one else would and giving them a chance to thrive and grow not only changed their lives for the better but made me realize just how fragile these little souls really are. Never in my wildest dreams could I have imagined that over a fifteen-year period I would take the wildest, yet most fulfilling, courageous, knowledgeable journey of my life rescuing two hundred puppies that came from unthinkable circumstances only to watch them grow into amazing dogs and go to wonderful homes. I have chosen to write about the most memorable stories that will stick with me for the rest of my life. I hope this book will be as remarkable for you to read as it was for me to write—as I feel
to have been touched by these amazing puppies and their tales of courage, resilience and heartbreak. They saved me as much as I saved them. And I feel honored to memorialize their stories in a book to share with the world.

I grew up in a small town in Texas named La Marque just south of Houston. I was born into a very religious family with loving parents, two older sisters, Yvonne and Betty, and an older brother, Jerry. I was the baby. Yvonne and Betty were like mothers to me and loved to take care of me. My brother, Jerry, was so proud of his little sister—he once took me to show and tell at school. We were such a very close family with tons of aunts, uncles and cousins spread out across the southwestern United States spanning all the way from Florida to Oklahoma.

I first went to church when I was *6 days old*. I attended the Vacation Bible

1

School every summer. I sang in the choir. I went on church retreats as a teenager. I have always loved church–loving and living for God–but most of all caring for others was something that both my parents instilled in us at a very young age.

My father was the Godliest man I have ever known. He lived to serve Jesus, he had a heart of gold, and never–not once–did he hesitate to open our doors to anyone in need. Be it financial, emotional, or even spiritual, my father lived to help others. It wasn't uncommon for people in our community who'd fallen on bad luck to stay at our house for a short spell until they'd landed back on their feet.
I suppose that's odd nowadays given how the concept of community has evolved (and in my view deteriorated), but when I was young there were no fences, backyards were shared, and it was expected that neighbors would help each other.

I remember watching with a careful eye as my dad would counsel those staying with us. "It's going to be okay," he'd say even if it wasn't. But his tone, reassuring as it was, just made them believe that everything would work itself out. There's a power to being caring and kind–there's a strength that grows out of compassion. And through my father I witnessed this at a young age, and I believe it's stuck with me ever since.

When I graduated high school, I wanted to spread my wings and move away from Texas. My brother, Jerry, and his wife lived in California. They offered me a nanny position to move in with them and take care of my nephew, and I jumped at the opportunity. I lived with Jerry and Cindy for about a year, then moved out and began working odd jobs here and there until eventually I returned just in time to witness the birth of their second son, Adam. I helped with Adam and Jamie until I got a great opportunity to work for General Telephone.

General Telephone was a massive company and my first grown up job in an age before computers and cell phones–notepads and xerox machines ruled the day. I enjoyed it, and I was good at it. While working at General Telephone I got married and had my daughter, Jessica. Life was chugging along smoothly until I had my first stroke of bad luck: my father who'd had a history of heart issues had taken a turn for the worse and now was gravely ill in a battle for his life.

I was able to take three months maternity leave to take care of him since I'd just recently given birth to my daughter. I stayed with him every night and held his hand in the same way he'd held countless others—only this time, I knew things weren't going to be fine: his condition was terminal, and he wasn't long for this world. I prayed each night for God to leave him on this earth long enough to meet his granddaughter and those prayers were answered: for four precious months he got to hold Jessica before he passed away.

We were all devastated at the loss but no one more so than my mom—she'd lost her best friend and was now alone. I remember sitting on the bed consoling her when she asked if I would leave her too and return to California. Seeing her in this weakened state had a profound impact on me. I couldn't contemplate leaving her now: she needed me. I didn't know how, but I would find a way to stay with her.

I called General Telehone fully expecting to be let go, but to my surprise they showed complete compassion to my situation, extending my maternity leave another three months on the spot without hesitation. Those three months were a godsend allowing me to care for my mom and allow her to spend time with Jessica. When the time finally came for us to return to California, she was back on her feet and getting stronger every day.

By the time I was back in California, it had been eight months, and I was pregnant with my first son, Daniel. When he was born, the cost of placing both my children in daycare was insurmountable, eating up most of my monthly paycheck. I thought to myself, *what if I do this myself?* I could take care of Daniel and Jessica and other kids and offer other parents in my position a more affordable option that wouldn't leave them penniless at the end of the month. It was a tough decision to leave General Telephone, because they had been so supportive of me, but I felt pulled into this path of caring for others. I gave my notice and opened up an in-home daycare center, aptly named Penny's Playhouse.

"Playhouse" it may have been for the kids, but it was no walk in the park for me. Taking care of children is not easy or enjoyable all the time– it's hard, all–consuming work that leaves you exhausted each day. I cared for fourteen children in my home *seven days a week* for six full years with babies as young as six weeks old and toddlers up to four. To have a baby that depends on you, *that needs you to survive*, is a tremendous responsibility and deep pleasure–even if it leaves you depleted. My mom came to visit in the summer when Jessica and Daniel were both six and five, and after taking one look at me she said it was time to move on: time to find a job in the real world again away from kids.

I immediately saw her point. As much as I loved kids, I needed to be around adults again. Plus, both my children were soon to start school and there wasn't the same need for Penny's Playhouse as before. It had served a purpose, but I needed to move forward. So, I closed the daycare center and began to work in a random assortment of assistant jobs that spanned the full spectrum of the rainbow: a real estate attorney, a property manager–an executive assistant in a furniture store, to the manager of a technology company–whoever needed assistance Penny was there. Many jobs had come and went, but there came a point where I felt as though I was just going through the motions again this time in the corporate world. It was a spiritual exhaustion and increasingly I wasn't very happy with where I was and saw no future where I was headed.

That's when I met John.

John had been a friend for ages who came back into my life after I'd been divorced for a few years from my first husband. With all the whirling winds surrounding me, John brought stability. He took care of us–of me and the kids. He had a great job with the Chevron Refinery that allowed us to breathe financially and gave me the space to focus on work that I really wanted to do. *What did I want to do? What work would give my life meaning?* I'd been bouncing from job to job, I'd never had the time to really ask myself that question, I'd just kept going.

RETIRING IN CABO

Soon after we were married, John and I took our first vacation to Cabo San Lucas, a resort city at the southern tip of the baja peninsula in Mexico. Cabo, as it's known for short, first became popular with Hollywood celebrities after

WWII, who would sneak away from the spotlight to enjoy exotic sports fishing jaunts in privacy. In the 1980s, the first hotels were built which led to a global interest, and within a decade world class resorts were popping up skyrocketing the sleepy town to national prominence as Mexico's premiere tourist destination spot.

I had never been to a place like Cabo. I remember pulling up in the taxi, stepping into the hotel lobby and being at a loss for words. The beautiful tiles, everything so clean and shiny–through the lobby you could see the pool and beyond that extended the vast ocean at sunset. Once in our room, John opened the curtains and Land's End–the rock formation that marks the meeting point between the Pacific Ocean and the Sea of Cortez–was right there, standing right in front of us. I immediately broke down and started crying–it was the most beautiful place I'd ever seen.

But it wasn't just the beauty of the place, the beauty was also in the people. Material things seemed unimportant. The kids in their tattered clothes, wearing shoes that didn't match, but they were always smiling. Everyone we met–in the restaurants, in the town–they were happy despite how little they had. The buildings, in 1997, were built with a bucket, a piece of rope, and a broken wheelbarrow. They didn't have the big machinery they have now, and yet everything seemed to work in harmony–better in a way than what I was used to in California.

I don't think I stopped smiling the entire ten days we were there. Something inside me knew this wasn't just a vacation; I'd found my home. I spoke to John about it and we both agreed–we would move here when we could.

By this time, I had been divorced for a few years and I was dating my now husband, John. I prayed for a job that would meet my expectations and would become available and my prayers were answered when I was offered a job at the Hilton Corporate Office in Beverly Hills. It was my dream job. By now Jessica was in college and Daniel was a fireman. John worked at the Chevron Refinery, and I was finally pleased with where my life was heading.

John and I loved to take vacations once or twice a year and we loved going to Cabo San Lucas, Mexico. We had no desire to go anywhere else, but Cabo and we often talked about someday possibly retiring there when the time was right.

Fast forward four years and the time was right. The kids were young adults and off on their own careers. John was ready to retire, and I was assured a job at the Los Cabos Hilton Resort in Cabo. We took a trip down to Cabo and met with a realtor, looking at different neighborhoods and homes. We wanted a neighborhood on the ocean side of the highway, a gated community with great security, a small house with a pool and garage or garage area. Our realtor showed us a fixer-upper house in our price range in the perfect neighborhood. It was 3 miles outside of town, which was perfect. The house had an ocean view as requested. The pool needed repairs and the inside of the house needed a lot of TLC but we were able to do the work ourselves. The price was right. We bought the house that day. It was going to take a while to finalize the paperwork, so we went back to California and a month later we flew down and signed the papers and just like that we were homeowners in Cabo San Lucas, Mexico. The next step was to take care of things in California and prepare for our move which was going to be in about 6-9 months. John submitted for his retirement and continued to work until it was finalized. I continued to work for another six months. I needed a work visa to work in Mexico, but I was assured that would all be taken care of once we moved.

The time had finally come for us to make the big move. We had a big going away party and said goodbye to all our friends. I had been packing for months and we had rented a U-Haul, loaded it up and took it down to the shipping company in San Diego. Daniel and John were going to drive my car down packed with things we would need in the house until the moving truck made it to Cabo. Cabo has a very small local newspaper called The Gringo Gazette. You can read it online. I was able to get a lot of things done through contacts in the newspaper before we even moved into our house like transferring our Dish Network and Vonage phone so we could have American TV and keep our US phone number. Our realtor had set up our utilities and internet.

Daniel and John took off 3 days before I flew out. When I got to the airport with my one large suitcase, I'll never forget the lady at the ticket counter asking me if I was excited about my vacation. I told her I wasn't going on vacation but was *actually* moving there. I think that's when it hit me that I was on my way to a new, huge, exciting yet scary adventure of a lifetime. This was final. There was no turning back now.

The funny thing is we had only seen the house twice: first, when we said we wanted to buy it and then again when we came to sign the papers. When we arrived, the house seemed so much smaller than we remembered. But the ocean view was beautiful with lots of cactuses and palm trees. There was an arroyo right across the street which was plush and green. The air was so clean and the sky so blue—we had arrived in Paradise. It was time for our new adventure to begin.

So here we were, living in Cabo and loving life. The first few months didn't come without their challenges. Language was a huge barrier as neither of us spoke Spanish other than a few words here and there. When we'd come on vacation, we would take a taxi if we wanted to go somewhere. Now we were on our own navigating around town. As luck would have it, they were remodeling the downtown and repaving the streets, so it seemed like every time we went to town, we had to take a detour. We got around well on our own and found some places we probably would never have found in a taxi going from the resort to the restaurant. John had to make a couple of trips back to California to bring down his truck, fishing gear and close some loose ends in California. But we were here to stay, and we were both so excited.

After a month or so we settled in, enough for me to start working at the Los Cabos Hilton Resort. After working in the Corporate Office for several years I was excited to start this new adventure at the beautiful resort. I did not have a work visa completed yet, so I moved around to different departments. Eventually I was moved to the Sales and Events office. I was very familiar with this department because I'd worked in Sales and Events at the Corporate Office in California. One downside was if the event went until 1:00 am I had to be there until 1:00 am. Then I would have to drive home on a dark, desert highway that had no streetlights and often cattle would come down from the hills and sleep on the warm pavement. It was often very challenging driving home—especially at night. I also had to work Saturdays with only one day off per week. After six months, I told John this was not my vision when we made the decision to move to Cabo—I simply wasn't enjoying myself. So, I approached the General Manager at the resort to see if I could possibly go part time but sadly that wasn't an option. After six months I resigned, sad to leave the work, the people and the property, but unable to keep up with the schedule.   I wasn't in any rush to find a new job. If something came along that sounded interesting, I would consider it; but for now, I was resolved to relax, breathe, and start enjoying beautiful Cabo.

1 VINCENTE

After being in Cabo for a few months, we noticed everyone had a dog. Unlike California, every time we went to a restaurant, marina, beaches, dogs seemed to be welcomed everywhere. And so, barely settled into our home,we made the decision that perhaps a dog should be part of our family.

I personally didn't have a lot of experience with dogs. I knew we had a cocker spaniel named Smokey when I was a baby, but I could only remember him from pictures: he passed away before I could remember him. My children had a Golden Retriever named Rusty early in their lives but when our living situation changed, Rusty went to live with a good friend who lived in Northern California. John had a Cocker Spaniel when we started dating but sadly he passed away shortly after. That was the sum-total of my past experience with dogs.

I really didn't know what we wanted. Did we want a puppy? Did we want an older dog? Big? Small? We decided we would just take a drive to the Los Cabos Humane Society and check out the dogs there to see if anything caught our attention. At that time the Humane Society was just a huge, fenced yard with a huge tree right in the middle and a small office. It was hot, humid, smelly and the flies were ridiculous. The dogs were all together running free in this dirt yard apart from a quarantine area off to the side. We walked in, and it was overwhelming. Big dogs ran up to greet us. Small dogs were chewing on our shoes. Some dogs jumped up to get petted. It was sad to see so many dogs there all wanting to come home with us.

We walked around, each going our separate ways to see if any dog looked like it would fit into our family. I noticed, sitting under a tree, a small little dog, who I'd later discover was a Corgie/Daschund mix. His tail was wagging and the closer I got to him the faster his tail would wag. Then his whole little body was wiggled with excitement. I sat down and started talking to him and he began licking me all over. I yelled to John, "I think I found one!" We hadn't been there very long but I was sure this little guy was the one for us. I picked him up and asked one of the volunteers his story. She told me that he was a surrender by a couple that was moving out of Cabo and could not take him with them. They said he was about 8 months old. He had all his shots and was fixed already. He weighed 13 lbs. I asked his name and he was named Vicente. He was in great health. He had these short little legs and ears that would stand straight up when you talked to him. I couldn't figure out why someone would get a dog then 8 months later take him to the Humane Society and not try to rehome him with a family. He had to be scared to death to come from a home and now in this huge yard with all these strange dogs. It broke my heart.

John and I decided that Vicente would be a perfect fit for our family. We sat with him for a little while in the office, and I could sense he was happy that we'd picked him. He loved sitting in my lap and licking my face. We filled out the adoption papers, paid the adoption fee, and just like that we'd adopted our first dog.

Once we got him in the car, we were both smiling ear to ear. We hadn't expected to find a dog so quickly and we hadn't prepared our home for a new family member, so we stopped by the pet store and got all the essentials: a dog bed, toys, collar and leash and food. When we got him home it was as if he'd lived with us forever. He went straight to his bed and laid down. He was completely house broken. He played with the toys, ran zoomies around the house and yard—we absolutely loved him, and I could tell by the way he stared at us with complete gratitude that he loved us too.

Vincent was a great addition to Casa Spade, our newly renamed home in Cabo. We found an amazing vet, Samantha, who owned the Animal Care Clinic, and she would become our vet going forward. Little did we or Vicente know that he would end up being a big brother and foster brother to 198 puppies and one cat that would make their way through Casa Spade over the next 15 years. He had so much patience with all the puppies, yet he didn't hesitate to put the puppies in their place when they got too rowdy rough housing. He really bonded closely with John. He and John went everywhere together. He loved going for walks and car rides, however Vicente did not like the pool. I would take him in the pool in the summer just to cool him off during Cabo's hot summers, but he would not voluntarily go in. If he could speak, Vicente would have many stories to tell about Casa Spade, but sadly, in 2020, we lost Vincente to heart disease. He brought so much joy and happiness to our home. He is—and will always be--truly missed.

2 MARLIN, SASSY, & LUCY

Before moving to Cabo, I was reading the Gringo Gazette online and read about a women's networking group called "The Los Cabos Tomatoes" which met every third Thursday of the month at a restaurant, new housing development, or resort. The owner of the business would invite the women to come to the establishment, take a tour of the development, and enjoy appetizers and cocktails while listening to local musicians and networking amongst each other. I knew I wanted to check out this women's group once I got settled in Cabo.

After grocery shopping one morning, I picked up a Gringo Gazette outside the store and noticed that there was going to be a Tomatoes meeting that afternoon at a new housing development right next to our neighborhood. It was time for me to get out and meet some local people, and this sounded like the perfect opportunity.

The meeting was scheduled from 3-5:30PM. Arriving early to pre-register, I noticed a girl sitting outside on the patio crying. I was curious but thought it best not to interfere and proceeded inside to complete my registration. Once inside, I received my badge. The tour began and finished–I grabbed my plate of appetizers and walked outside, still drawn to this girl who'd been crying. Sitting down next to her, I introduced myself as Penny and asked why she was crying. Her name was Katy, and she was a dog rescuer in Cabo. Taking out a teeny, tiny puppy from the kennel sitting on the floor next to her, she told me she'd been awoken this morning by the sounds of three puppies left by her front door in a box by someone who didn't want them anymore.

As a rescuer she often found dogs outside her home, but this time she couldn't take them in with everything else she had going on in her life. She needed to find them a foster home and hoped that could happen at this meeting. Handing me one of the puppies, I noticed its eyes had not yet opened, and I melted. I had never held anything so tiny and helpless. It infuriated me that someone could have left such fragile and innocent souls in a box—just left them at someone else's doorstep. How cruel! Katy said she was hoping to find someone to foster the puppies at this meeting because she could not take them back home with her. I was intrigued as to exactly what she meant by fostering. After all, I was not working at the time, and I loved caring for people, how difficult could it be to care for little puppies?

I proceeded to question her as to what all fostering entailed. She said they needed to be bottle fed for at least four to six weeks. I remember when I had my home daycare one of my favorite times was bottle feeding a new baby and falling asleep in my arms. That was very relaxing to me. Now I was definitely interested in these little babies. We talked for at least an hour right there on the couch, while I was holding these tiny little babies estimated to be around thirteen days old, According to Katy puppies eyes open around 17-19 days. She told me about how long she'd lived in Cabo, how she got into rescuing dogs and how rewarding it was. She also told me if she couldn't find someone to foster these puppies that she would be forced to take them to the shelter and they might not survive because they were so tiny and needed around the clock attention for at least the next 3 weeks. After our visit to the shelter when we got Vicente I couldn't imagine these 3 tiny little beings out there in the heat and dirt and flies. It broke my heart. There was no way I was going to let these puppies go there. Katy informed me she had the bottles and formula in her car. The puppies were already in a kennel—she just needed someone to take them home and bottle feed them until they were old enough to eat on their own and then they could get adopted.

At this point I had already known in my heart that these puppies were coming home with me. They had stolen my heart. I told her I would do it. She started crying even harder and asked, "are you sure?"

I figured I had nowhere I had to be, nothing I had to do and how hard could it be? John loves animals—he wouldn't mind. I didn't meet anyone else at the meeting, I didn't speak with anyone else—the entire time I spoke to Katy. The decision was made. I would take these puppies home and foster them until they were old enough to be adopted. Katy would walk me through everything, check up on me and if I needed anything she was only a phone call away. We left the meeting, loaded up the kennel with the puppies, and they came straight home to Casa Spade.

Pulling into my driveway with Katy behind me, Vicente was already at the gate ready to greet us. I parked the car and grabbed the kennel from Katy's car when Vincent proceeded to go nuts. He could smell and hear the puppies crying. Zooming around the yard he could hardly contain himself knowing our family of canines had just tripled. John's eyes lit up and he carefully asked what did I have with me. Pulling out just one puppy and placing it into his arms, John smiled from ear to hear cradling the newborn and starting to give it kisses. Then I took out another. "There's two?" He said confused. Then I took out a third. "Oh my goodness," he exclaimed. "Oh my goodness." Vincente had returned from his zooming and sat exasperated, his tail still wagging as he smelled his new siblings.

I introduced Katy to John and explained the situation that Katy needed someone to foster these little puppies until they were old enough to get adopted. To be honest, I was nervous not knowing what we were taking on, but John's excitement put me at ease. Little did we know we had just signed up for something that would become our lives for the next fifteen years.

While John held the puppies on the couch Katy followed me into the kitchen and proceeded to show me how to prepare a bottle of formula. The bottles were so tiny they could be mistaken for Barbie miniatures—they reminded me of the ones my daughter Jessica used with her dolls as a little girl. Preparing the formula was similar to human baby formula so that part was easy. Katy then showed me how to feed the puppies. Never having fed a baby animal before, I felt totally clueless. Unlike a human baby which you hold in your arms on their back, puppies are fed in your lap while flat on their bellies with the bottle out in front of them. It might seem insignificant, but it's a totally different feel and took some adjusting to get the bottle in the first puppy's mouth. What I remember most is how without the use of its eyes or ears, it had to smell the bottle and squirm his little body into position, his head moving back and forth until his tiny lips made contact. Only then, when his tiny lips found the nipple and started sucking on it did I finally relax, sweating with anxiety.

After a few minutes of feeding, he needed to be burped. Yes, puppies need to be burped too in order to release the air bubbles. So upon my shoulder lie this little puppy I was rubbing and gently padding to make sure it would burp. I couldn't help but feel moved. Yes, he also pooped and peed all over my shirt, but in that moment I felt the same connection I had missed for so many years. My need to care for others—other souls non-human, it didn't matter. I needed another soul to need me, to depend upon me in the same way that my own babies had—for life.

I smiled at John and sent him out to get some yellow shop towels to clean up

15

the mess the puppy had made. Gently returning him to his kennel, I reached for the second puppy and repeated the process: feeding, burping except this time with more confidence. By the time I started with the third I was a pro. I can't remember how long it took to feed all three. It seemed like an hour, but really it was probably only about twenty-five minutes. I looked at John and confirmed with him if he thought we could do this? He said it's up to me because I was the one that was going to be bottle feeding, every two to four hours all night long. It then hit me, I'm going to have to get up all night long and feed these little puppies every night for the next month until they could eat on their own. What have I gotten myself into? The puppies now had full bellies and were sleeping soundly in the kennel.

Katy hung around for a while longer, telling me how long she had lived in Cabo and how she got into rescuing dogs. She had no less than six dogs at her house at any time looking for homes. I remember when John and I would come down on vacation that there seemed to be several stray dogs around the resort and occasionally walking the streets in town. But there was a whole part of Cabo that we didn't even know about. There were barrios outside of the tourist areas, three miles outside of town, where thousands of dogs were out there just running the streets alone. I couldn't believe it. I'd come from California where everyone keeps their dogs in yards. This was shocking to me. Little did I know then that I too would become a part of those rescuing dogs from these barrios—volunteering at spay and neuter clinics, catching strays from the highway, at the gas station, at Costco and Walmart. Having a kennel, leashes, water bowls and dog treats would become the new normal in my car.

But for now, my focus was on these three little babies and keeping them alive. Katy suggested I use the Gringo Gazette newspapers for the bottom of the kennel. I sent John to the market to grab a stack of those. I had a whole can of powdered formula and we had several yellow shop towels, so I was set. Katy seemed confident in what she had seen so far from me, and so off she went.

After she left, the weight of everything that happened began to sink in. I needed something to do, and in that moment it hit me that this may be exactly what I was missing. I was a caregiver, and not only had I missed that, but there was a void that had been created in its absence. I was meant to do this. I knew that as I held these puppies, and they began to cry. It was time for another feeding. At this time they were only drinking about an ounce or two each, so I only had to make one more bottle from the powdered formula, and they all shared. Then it was bedtime.

The first night was a sleepless night for me. It wasn't so much the puppies waking me up, but me worrying that I wouldn't wake up to feed them. I should have known I needn't worry about that—any tender newborn in need of food will let you know. Three hungry puppies all crying at once is impossible to sleep through. So just as Katy had forewarned, I was up every two to three hours feeding these puppies and getting more relaxed as the days went by. I was getting better at burping and using the baby wipes to bathe them. Every feeding I'd clean out their kennel with new paper and put a couple of really soft baby blankets in the kennel for them to sleep; however they preferred to sleep on top of each other in a pile.

On the fifth day their eyes first opened. This meant they were nineteen days old and ready to be taken for their first trip to the vet. I took them to Samantha who she'd also worked with and would make sure they were gaining weight, and I was doing everything I needed to keep these puppies alive. They weighed approximately three pounds each by now more than doubling their weight since I first started feeding them. Samantha gave them their first deworming shot at that visit and told me to bring them back two weeks later for the second one. She assured me they were adorable, healthy, and urged me to keep doing what I was doing.

I brought them home and I was officially a proud foster mom to my first three puppies. I absolutely loved it. I was in my element. Now that they could see me and see the bottle, when feeding time came it got a lot easier. Seeing a puppy's eyes open for the first time is magical. Before when you feed them it's a whole different feeling; now, when you pick them up, they stare at you. They see the nipple of the bottle and when sucking they look into your eyes. A week later their ears open and they begin to hear you. They start walking in a straight line instead of aimlessly in circles. They hear you when you call them. It's simply magical watching these teeny, tiny, little beings come to life and grow into puppies from balls of fur. Two of the puppies were just that: brown balls of fur, a little girl and a little boy. The third puppy, a little girl, was solid white with short hair. They began to scoot around in circles when I'd take them out of the kennel. I set up baby gates to confine them to a small area, so they had more room to move around. I was starting to feel very proud of what I had accomplished. I had kept these little babies alive who most likely would have never made it had I not met Katy at the Tomatoes meeting and agreed to go on this adventure. It's natural to feel a sense of pride for that and it filled me with joy.

The three puppies were thriving and growing daily. They were starting to now try and walk and fall over. They were adorable. I bought a play yard, which gave them more room to move around and set it up in the living room under the window, so they could get a nice ocean breeze and enjoy the morning sunshine. It also allowed them to see us and Vincente as well as hear the TV. Many Gringo Gazette newspapers were soiled before we finished the third can of powdered formula, but we were doing great. I loved them so much. Every day was something new and exciting with them. We were all growing together: I learned their needs and they learned that I was there for them if they needed anything.

Soon, they were starting to growl at each other and chew on each other which would make whomever was being attacked cry. When I would call, them they would try their best to run over to me at the edge of the play yard. Now the two brown ones were huge balls of long fur. They had yellow eyes. They looked like they could be part Husky. The male loved to play in the water bowl and make a huge mess. For that reason, we decided to name him Marlin. Marlin is a very popular fish in Cabo that people come down to catch, so Marlin seemed right for the boy. The little girl had such a wiggle in her butt when she walked, she seemed perfect for Sassy. Then there was the short haired, white little girl. How on earth did she end up in that box with these two big, fluffy, long haired other puppies who were now much bigger than her? There was a lot of explaining to do. We ended up naming her Lucy like Lucille Ball because Ricky was always telling Lucy she has some explaining to do—just as little Lucy had some explaining to do as to how she ended up with Marlin and Sassy. What I hadn't yet learned yet is that a female dog in heat can have several partners leading to a litter that contains several different breeds, sizes and colors. Oftentimes the puppies never know who their true parents really are!

My three babies were now close to six weeks old. We made our third visit to Samantha and she gave them their first puppy shot and second deworming. She then told me that I could start giving them puppy mush. I had no idea what puppy mush was. It turns out puppy mush is dry puppy food in a blender with formula. I was buying my puppy food from Samantha because it was high grade, full of vitamins and minerals. Going forward that's what all my puppies would eat until they left my home. Samantha told me to make it like a watery oatmeal and put in a pie tin. I thought to myself this was going to be a piece of cake. Bye-bye bottle feeding, hello normal meals! Well, it was much easier to feed them, however, like a smash cake you give a one year old on their birthday celebration. I put down some newspaper, put the pie tin in the middle and let them have it. OMG I don't know if any of the mush made it into their bellies but I do know that every nook and cranny and crevice of their body had mush on it. They were walking through the pie tin. Falling over in the pie tin. They were licking mush off of each other. Eventually the pie tin was empty and all three looked like I had rolled them in cake batter! This is when John and I started tag teaming. I had to take each puppy, one by one and give it a bath while John made sure the other two would stay on the paper, or close to it. Then I would hand him the clean puppy, and I would grab puppy number two until we finally had given all three a bath. After their baths, I would put them into a nice, clean play yard and they would literally pass out with full bellies. It was as if they were drugged. Puppy mush would knock them out and they could sleep through anything. At this point they were only getting mush once a day. The other feedings were still bottle feedings. After about a week, they were promoted to two mush feedings and eventually all their meals were mush. They were starting to get these little razor teeth coming in too so the mush would have a little thicker consistency to it and they weren't making as much of a mess. Eventually they graduated to teeny, tiny little dry food because now they could actually chew.

At 10 weeks old they got their second puppy shot. They had been dewormed twice now, had their second puppy shot and were not having any formula anymore. What this meant was they just needed one more puppy shot then they could find 4ever homes and could get adopted. It still makes me cry to think that they were all going to be leaving Casa Spade. I had bought all three stuffed animals. I kept them in the play yard with the puppies so it would have the smell of each other or at least a familiar smell on them when they went to their new homes.

At ten weeks they got their last puppy shot and were officially able to go to their new homes. Katy ended up taking Sassy to LaPaz with her when she went for a weekend in hopes that someone would adopt her. She took her vaccination book, blanket and toy and off she went but not without me balling my eyes out. I was going to miss her so much. She was so tiny when I first met Katy at that Tomatoes meeting and now she weighed nearly ten pounds and was so beautiful with her long, brown hair and yellow eyes. I knew she was in good hands with Katy, afterall, Katy had been rescuing for years and taught me how to be a foster mom. Luckily Katy was successful in finding a family for Sassy at the resort she stayed at. The family was from Sacramento and fell in love with her. So one puppy down two to go to find 4ever homes.

We had some friends here that we'd met when we first moved to Cabo. They had some friends visiting from Canada whom they had told about these two puppies I had been fostering who needed new homes. One afternoon they brought them over to meet the puppies and the husband, Kevin, fell in love with Lucy. She was tiny, graceful like a little white deer and such a beautiful little girl. They were looking for a new dog but hadn't really considered adopting a puppy let alone a puppy from Mexico. But Kevin was in love. They made the decision to take her to their condo for an overnight stay to see if they bonded with her, and the rest was history. They definitely wanted to adopt her. I gave Babe and Kevin her vaccination book, blanket and stuffed animal, and gave her kisses. Same as with Sassy tears were shed and off she went to eventually go home to Canada. Lucy had a twelve hour flight home and didn't make a sound the whole flight. She was an angel. They did mention when they got home she was very scared. New men scared her. She absolutely hated fireworks but loved chasing her Kong toy in the backyard. Lucy loved to cuddle with her dad on the couch. Like Vicente with John Lucy and her dad bonded and were inseparable. At nine years old she started having difficulty breathing. The vet was unsure what the problem was until they did an XRay. That's when they found a tumor on her spleen. Kevin and Babe were devastated. They decided to do palliative care, making her comfortable as long as they could. It was ultimately Kevin's decision to let her go. As of this writing she has been gone for five years. Nobody will ever forget that strawberry freckled faced dog. She was one in a million.

Now we just had Marlin left. During this time John was still going back and forth to California and I was left home alone for a week at a time. Marlin by this time was huge. He was growing like crazy although still a gentle giant. He wouldn't hurt a fly but had never met a stranger. Big and furry, he would bark whenever anyone would walk past the yard. He loved swimming in the pool. He loved swimming in the ocean. He was my swimming partner and got so excited whenever I started putting on my bathing suit. He would put one foot in the pool and look back to make sure it was okay for him to go in and make sure I was coming. We have a seat step in the pool and sometimes he would be so relaxed I would catch him dozing off while standing on the step. Marlin was definitely a water dog and his name fit him perfectly.

He and Vicente got along so well we made the decision to keep him. In the rescue world that's called a "foster fail". He was going to be my protector even though I did not feel threatened in any way in our home. Marlin was so beautiful. We later figured out he was probably part Husky and Australian Shepherd. He had this golden mane around his neck. His tail was long and had long hair like a horse. His eyes were golden. Wherever we went, people would compliment Marlin on how beautiful and gentle he was. He loved children and other dogs and was never aggressive—such an amazing big foster brother to all the other puppies that came through Casa Spade. Sadly, at the age of 15 he started having seizures that were uncontrollable with medication. That with his arthritis made it difficult for him to get up and down the stairs, not to mention lying down. He was never a dog bed dog which might have helped prevent or treat his arthritis. Instead he loved to lay on the tile floors or even outside, in the heat, on the tiles around the pool—always on the cool tiles. With his arthritis and seizures, he was in too much pain. So we made the hard decision to let him cross the rainbow bridge. In doggie vocabulary that's going to doggie heaven. I loved him so much. He was so big and sweet and there is still such a void in this house without him running around or swimming in the pool.

So for three months, we had successfully fostered and raised three adorable puppies and found them great 4ever homes. These first three would lead to one hundred and ninety-seven more. Obviously, I cannot write about all two hundred puppies, but I will try to offer the most heart-wrenching, heartwarming, happy-ending stories I think you'll appreciate, and which helped me grow in the process learning as much about myself as I did them in the brief but magical time we shared together.

3 LIDIA

Cabo is known to have inclement weather during the summer and fall, the worst arriving between September and November. One September, a tremendous tropical storm arrived which caused as much damage as a hurricane and left Cabo flattened and in disarray. The name they gave this storm was Lidia.

Lidia brought more water and mud than wind damage. The water came down from the mountains with such a force, it literally, along the way, wiped out entire neighborhoods. It took people's homes that were made out of tins. It washed away cars, dealerships, animals, roads, buses, utility poles, boats—whatever lay in her path between the mountains and the ocean was wiped clean. It even took a lady's children who were standing next to her and washed them with the force of the mud out into the ocean. The damage Lidia wreaked on our little town was inconceivable but worst of all, nobody was prepared for it.

When tragedy strikes in Mexico, a curious thing happens. The community springs into action with a wide network to provide help and support to those in need. Not to disparage the government agencies—they do their best; but it's people, everyday people, who, in these tragic situations, tend to stand taller exhibiting the quiet heroism that's not only inspiring to witness but inspires one to action. Lidia was one of those times where the community needed to come together to help those who had literally lost everything. And so volunteers would meet and gather essential food and water supplies, clothing and toiletries and assemble care packages for both humans and animals. Once the care packages were assembled, we would then embark on the humbling journey of delivering this assistance to those now living in a wasteland.

Volunteers would go out the day before and distribute tickets to all those who had been affected in the areas we would be visiting the next day. In the morning we'd pile into 4 Wheel drive vehicles and ATVs, the only vehicles capable of navigating the broken-down roads, and search for those standing in line holding their tickets. I was always so impressed how patient and organized the people were. They would stand in lines, no pushing or shoving and patiently wait until their turn came. Often restaurants would make big pots of spaghetti and we'd give the people a plate of food along with their supplies. It was extremely well-orchestrated, and we did this several times per week until the people regained some stability in their lives.

I was at one of those homes assembling care packages when a call came through from a lady who had literally stumbled upon a huge hole full of mud. To her astonishment in that hole was a mama dog and her six puppies. Tragically five of the six puppies were already dead, but one was barely alive. She was able to remove the mama dog from the hole but the puppy's condition was grave. The home owner asked if I might be interested in rescuing this puppy, and of course I said, "yes, absolutely".

The entire highway and town was torn up and covered with mud, so taking the injured pup to Samantha wasn't an option. The lady showed up with this tiny, tiny less than a pound puppy in horrible condition that was wheezing and having a difficult time breathing. I brought her home and the first thing I did was give her a warm bath to get all the mud off of her and to see exactly what kind of condition she was in. Once I got her cleaned other than being very thin and dehydrated she looked ok but was definitely having trouble with each breath. I gave her some warm formula and just held her. I Face Timed with Samantha, and she told me to just keep her warm and comfortable and bring her in first thing in the morning. But after a few hours she started having seizures—one seizure right after another. I didn't know what to do, so I called Samantha again, and she advised me to put honey on her gums and rub rubbing alcohol on her belly. Honey works as an insulin for animals in shock and the alcohol opens up the pores in the blood vessels to get the blood flowing. I nursed her like this throughout the night, fearing she wouldn't make it but praying to God that she would—knowing she'd have my very best effort to keep her alive. I carried her in my sports bra so she could feel my heartbeat to calm her and keep her warm.

By God's good grace, she survived the night along with several seizures, and when the morning came I knew I could waste no time but take her to see Samantha. Navigating our way through the mud and debris in town, we arrived safely, and Samantha quickly performed an emergency exam and set her on oxygen. Her lungs were full of fluid, so Samantha gave her a shot to help with

24

that but otherwise all we could do was sit and wait and hope for the best.

After what seemed like hours of treatment, Samantha said she was stable enough to bring her tiny little body home. I don't think I put her down more than ten minutes at a time only to feed her for the next few days. She pretty much was attached to me close to my heart. Surprisingly day by day she got a little better and stronger and eventually I knew she was going to survive. It was definitely touch and go though on several occasions for quite a while. With all she had been through I knew she needed a strong name and what better name than Lidia after the storm that almost took her life? Lidia continued to thrive. She was eating great and gaining weight. She was walking and playing with toys. She was just this white bundle of energy. Everyone who met her loved her and her tale of survival. We were stuck at home for quite a while due to the damage the storm had caused, but eventually I was able to take her out with me in a puppy sling or a puppy wagon for walks on the marina. She loved walks, and she loved people. She also loved swimming in the pool. She made several visits to Samantha to get her deworming and puppy shots and to reassure me she was doing better. Lidia's coat turned out to be brown and white like a deer. She still needed one more puppy shot and to get fixed before we could put her up for adoption. By now, she was close to 2 months old and doing amazing.

It was October, and I would always volunteer at the Humane Society Booth on the marina during the Bisbee Fishing Tournament held in Cabo that same month. We were surprised they were going to have it that year since the storm had caused so much damage to the town. But in true Mexican spirit, everyone rallies and gets things done. Before you know it, the town looked as it had before minus some missing buildings and telephone poles. Normally I would have puppies with me if I was fostering but after all that little Lidia had been through and the fact that she hadn't had all her puppy shots yet I thought it best to not let her come with me to the booth. There were so many people walking around the marina. Our booth sold t shirts, collars and leashes and welcomed donations. We also sold dog toys and treats. People often looked forward to our booth, and the marina was packed on this particular day, elbow to elbow with tourists in town for the tournament.

There was live music everywhere and tons of food booths. A lady who had been coming to the Bisbee tournament for years stopped by our booth in hopes that we would have puppies or kittens for her to pet. I hadn't brought any this year, but I did tell her of an adorable puppy at my house. I showed her some pictures of Lidia and she fell in love with her just from the pictures. She even sent pictures to her husband. Her name was Bunnie, we exchanged information, and honestly, I didn't think I would see her again. That happens a lot even when we would have animals in the booth. People would pet them and love them and want them, but then would never come back. But Bunnie seemed different. She was very interested and definitely wanted to meet her in person if she could. I scheduled a meet and greet with her in a few days at a local restaurant on the marina. She said she'd come and had already spoken about Lidia to her husband.

I didn't know much about Bunnie but she seemed like a nice lady so I put Lidia in my car and off to the marina we went to meet Bunnie. I walked up with Lidia in my puppy sling and everyone on the marina and in the restaurant were going crazy over her. I noticed Bunnie and her friend sitting at a table in the middle of the restaurant. Bunnie saw me with Lidia and she literally got up and ran over to me. It was love at first sight. Lidia loved Bunnie as well, giving her lots of kisses. I proceeded to tell Bunnie about Lidia's amazing survival story which made her love her even more. It only took a couple hours before she said she'd love to adopt her. I thought Bunnie would be the perfect fit for little Lidia however there were two huge issues with her adopting Lidia. One was that Lidia wasn't ready to be adopted yet. She still needed to finish her puppy vaccinations and she needed to be fixed. So she couldn't travel for at least another month. And if that wasn't enough, Bunnie lived in Philadelphia. I had been fostering a few years by then and my main connection where I sent my puppies was called Rescue Faerie run by Suzanne Hein Fountain and her husband, Tom, in Portland, Oregon. I had no contacts or escorts that went to the east coast. Escorts are people who would volunteer to take dogs on the plane with them to their destination and hand them over to the rescue organization or the person that was adopting them. I had nothing. I knew no one on the east coast at all.

So this was a bit of an issue. No matter how much Bunnie loved Lidia, I didn't think she would want to come back to Cabo in a month to pick her up. I wasn't in a position to fly her to Philadelphia either so it was feeling like Lidia wasn't going to have a 4ever home afterall. However, a true believer that God works miracles, I'd hoped He would find a way. A few minutes later, as we were discussing the dilemma, a lady sensed how distressed we were and came over to introduce herself as Shannon. Shannon couldn't help but overhear our conversation and as it happened was herself from Philadelphia. She'd planned on returning in a month and would be happy to escort Lidia to Bunnie if that would help.

How amazing! What were the odds? Thanks be to God. So Bunnie and

Shannon exchanged information. Shannon and I exchanged information. Bunnie officially adopted Lidia right there in the restaurant. We kept in touch throughout the month, and I would send Bunnie pictures and videos throughout the next month. Lidia finished up her vaccinations and got fixed. I bought her a brand new travel carrier, collar, leash and a fancy new outfit to travel on the plane with Shannon.

When the day finally arrived, I remember driving all the way to the airport in tears looking at Lidia peek her head out of her new kennel, showing off her little pink dress. Unable to control myself, I kept telling her how much I was going to miss her. Arriving at the airport, we parked, walked inside and looked around until we found Shannon. We sat at a restaurant and talked for a bit while I thanked her so much for what she was doing. When it was time for her to go upstairs with Lidia I held her and cried ugly. This little puppy that came to me as a half-pound muddy mess–that almost died several times the first night–she taught me to never give up. You pray to God with all your might that He will come through–and He did. And she did. Now she was big and healthy, going on her new journey with her new family, and it left me destroyed. The hardest part of fostering rescue puppies is when they touch your heart and still, you have to let them go.

I drove away from the airport that day in tears and it took me a while to recover. Still today when I see photos of Lidia I'm brought to tears but I quickly start to smile when I think of how happy she is being part of Bunnie's family. Lidia is now 7 years old. She is still full of spunk and loves to play with her toys and ball. She's always ready to go for a ride in the truck or car or take a hike in the woods. She has a twelve year old sister named Roxie. They play together, sleep together and are thick as thieves. She loves people but does not like other dogs. Bunnie says it's her alpha attitude. She loves laying in the hot sun, the hotter the better. Bunnie chalks this up to being a Cabo native. She is good at expressing her feelings with a stare, a head tilt and loves her voice. She loves to talk and always has a smile on her face. Lidia has grown to be a smart, loving and great companion. She is very loved. Bunnie and I have since kept in touch, and both she and her girlfriends return to Cabo every year. We will stay forever friends thanks to a tiny puppy with a huge heart that persevered, defied the odds, and found her forever home.

4 LUCAS

The most populated tourist beach in Cabo is called Medano. There are several restaurants, a couple of resorts and tons of vendors there on a daily basis. It can get pretty wild at times especially during spring break. One day a friend of mine, Mike, was down at Medano with his friends when he noticed a very intoxicated man walking along the beach carrying a puppy, dropping it, holding it by his hind legs—basically manhandling and mishandling this tiny puppy. Mike asked his friend to walk over to the man and offer him $500 pesos for the puppy, which at the time was about twenty-five dollars. The drunk said he would take $1,000 pesos. Mike gave his friend a $1,000 pesos to give to the man, and he relinquished the puppy. The poor puppy's eyes weren't even opened yet which meant he was less than nineteen days old.

Mike and his friend took the puppy to a restaurant down on the beach and they gave him a little bowl of milk, except he was too tiny to drink the milk. Mike told his friend, this is going to be your puppy, not mine. The friend said she was heading back to Canada the next day and therefore it was impossible for her to take the puppy. So they started searching elsewhere along the beach when they ran into a couple, Suzanne and John, on the way walking back to their resort. Showing them the puppy, Mike explained how they ended up together and began to discuss the situation when the puppy began peeing on Suzanne, presumably marking his territory. "He must want me to take him," Suzanne said, smiling at her husband. Well there was no way this puppy was going to leave Mexico for at least another two months, and Suzanne and John were on their way back to California the next day. They all exchanged information and hoped they could figure something out, but admittedly everyone agreed it was a long shot.

Since no one could physically take the puppy home, Mike's friend took the puppy to Samantha, who she knew already, and explained the situation: they had found a couple who wanted this poor puppy that'd been mistreated but who also needed a foster until he was old enough to travel. Of course I was going to get it. I drove to Samantha's office after receiving her call, picked up the puppy and told him, "it looks like you're going to be hanging out at Casa Spade for a bit," before bringing him home.

He was absolutely adorable. A little brown and white fur ball. I already had formula and bottles, pee pads which by this time I was now buying by the case at Costco. No more Gringo Gazettes, yellow towels and a play-yard, all the normal puppy outfitting necessities by this time in my home. I contacted Suzanne about a week later to confirm they indeed were interested in adopting him. I explained the responsibility of adopting a puppy from Mexico. First, since we didn't know who the mom or dad was, we had no idea how big he was going to be—we didn't even know what breed he was—as he was only about 17 days old. I also explained that he had been abused and sometimes that can affect the puppy's personality going forward even though he was so small. But Suzzane assured me they wanted him. I explained if at any time they changed their mind I could find another home for him, but again she said they definitely wanted him, and they'd already named him Lucas.

This was important, because as Lucas grew older he did indeed exhibit problems that were outside of his control. He hit all his milestones like a normal, healthy, happy puppy, however Lucas was a growler. Not a biter, just a growler—all four pounds of him. Growling indicates an inner-anxiety, a fear, or in Lucas' case: lingering residue from a past trauma. Being dropped on his head as a puppy by some uncaring man that was neither his mother nor father took a toll. We are all an accumulation of energy, the product of energies past, some buried deep and left unresolved. In those most precious first days when a newborn soul needs to be nurtured and loved by his parents, Lucas received anything but, and this gaping void was filled with growling.

With Lucas being the only puppy in my home at the time the only discipline he got was from me or my older dogs. So he had a little temper in him, but he was so tiny I was almost positive he was going to outgrow his growling before he went to Suzanne and John's. When he didn't I grew worried. He loved the pool, loved being outside, but the growling continued. I asked Samantha what to do and she suggested I growl back at him. So that's what I did. I growled back at him with love in the hopes that at some point he would realize there was no need to growl anymore. It got slightly better but was still there in his temperament as he continued to grow into a truly beautiful puppy. Lucas got all his puppy shots, was fixed and learned to walk on a leash. He learned to sleep in the play yard and even got spoiled by having free range of the house. Everything was on track save these underlying issues I was confident I could fix before he left Casa Spade.

When the time finally came for Lucas to go to his new home in California, it just happened that John and I had a trip scheduled to California just shy of thirty minutes from where Suzanne and John lived. I bought a new kennel for Lucas and of course he had his blanket and favorite stuffed animal. Lucas was a good little boy the entire flight to Los Angeles, sleeping the entire flight, not making a single peep.

We proceeded to the hotel we were staying and waited in the patio area outside the restaurant. I had never personally met Suzanne and John. I had no idea who we were looking for but I knew someone would eventually show up looking for a puppy. We weren't there for very long before they came. Just as he was handed over to Suzanne the first time, Lucas began to growl. I assured her he would outgrow it once he adapted to his new surroundings, but honestly at this point I wasn't so sure.

They took him home and as the growling persisted, it became necessary to take him to obedience classes. When that wasn't enough, a personal trainer came to the house. Nothing seemed to work until Lucas found his true calling as a watchdog. Amazingly by protecting others he was able to heal himself. Lucas was uncomfortable around older dogs but loved puppies. He loved to go on hikes on the trails behind his house. He loved protecting the family's cats. He takes food very gently from their fingers. John would take Lucas on long walks and he would even feel pride in protecting John. Now at almost fifteen he has slowed down. His hearing is fading and he sleeps a lot. But he still gets bursts of energy and will run around and play. They love him and he got very lucky to be rewarded with such loving parents.

Lucas has come a long way from that tiny little puppy manhandled at the beach in Cabo. He lives now in a beautiful home with a beautiful yard and he is very happy. I went to visit him several years ago and he still remembers me. To this day Suzanne and John are dear friends of ours and we see them often here in Cabo or if we go to California.

5 DOODLE

I was sitting at home one day just relaxing and watching tv when I got a call from another vet out at the Humane Society. She told me that a puppy was just brought in by a boat captain.

The captain was driving down the street when he saw someone throw out what appeared to be trash from his car window. But then he noticed the trash was moving, so he pulled over to take a closer look and it was clear the trash, in fact, was a very mangy, dirty, skinny puppy of about five months old. Picking him up, he rushed the puppy to the Humane Society, offering $500 pesos in the hopes that somebody could save him.

The vet checked him over and other than being malnourished and matted, he tested negative for any serious dog diseases. Nevertheless, he was so skinny, when the vet called me she wasn't sure whether he would make it and so didn't want to put him in a kennel for the night; rather, she'd hoped I would come and get him, so off to the shelter I went.

The dog was pitiful. He had a look in his eyes of being both lost, sad, and scared. With a Humane Society in town, how could a person throw him away like a piece of trash on the road? To me it was the lowest of the lows. What would surprise me even more is that this kind of ignominious introduction would become the norm of puppies passing through Casa Spade in the years to come, marking a failure of the human spirit that's still difficult for me to reconcile. Nevertheless, I wrapped him in a towel, put him in my front seat, and talked to him all the way home. "You're in good hands now, you're going to get better," I reassured him. "We're going to get you a bath and some food," I promised, hoping the act of cruelty he'd suffered hadn't left an indelible mark upon his spirit and soul.

When we arrived at Casa Spade, the first thing we did was take him outside and give him a good haircut. A dog-groomer I am not, but it was important to cut out all the matts in his fur as it seemed this puppy hadn't taken a bath his entire life. Next I gave him a bath, and that's when I lost it and began to cry inconsolably. He was literally skin and bones, set in between with patches of fur. It was incomprehensible he was still alive. I gathered myself and then gave him some high grade soft canned food of which he ate a little—much less than I expected—and promptly fell asleep.

About an hour later, he awoke suddenly and was immediately sick, vomiting violently with diarrhea so bad he could barely stand and support himself. I called Samantha who told me to bring him in immediately so she could take a look. Very quickly she noted he was suffering from dehydration, malnourishment and he needed to be put on an IV immediately to receive the missing fluids, vitamins and minerals. I asked her how long she thought he'd be there and to my astonishment she said a minimum of ten days.

I guess he was a lot worse off than I had guessed. That's how sick he was. But he had that look of hope in his eyes when I talked to him. I left him at the vet but I went and visited him every single day for nine days and he didn't seem to be improving. He would just lay there receiving the fluids but showing no other signs of life. I would pet him and talk to him and tell him he needed to get better, so he could come home. On the tenth day I went to the vet thinking this is the make it or break it day. He's going to be better or he's going to have to be put down. I walked in and asked how he was. She said look. I walked back to his kennel and he was standing up! I started crying. Samantha started crying. He was going to make it after all.

She couldn't believe it either but this little guy had the will to live and was going to make it. She said he's doing better, but she wanted to keep him for three more days just to make sure. So I went back two days in a row and on the third day I was able to bring the little guy home. I brought him home and though he was still skinny, he now had a little spunk to him. John looked at me and said, don't get attached because we are not keeping him. "Too late," I told him. "This little Doodle is staying right here." I hadn't thought about it—his name just came out at that moment—but he was a little doodle. A doodle of skin, fur and bones and the name perfectly fit his look and personality.

Slowly I started hand-feeding him little bits of food. I'd carry him out to the yard to do his business. It took a little over a month for this little Doodle Bug to show his personality but once he did, let me tell you, he was hilarious, sweet, loving—he was the best little dog ever. He loved to swim with his big brother Marlin. He loved his big brother Vincente. The three of them I'd take

35

out to dinner and they plop themselves right under the table, the patrons not even knowing they were there.

Doodle has now been part of this family for fifteen years and has witnessed one hundred and eighty puppies come through Casa Spade. He has touched everyone's heart. Now Doodle is going on sixteen and has Canine Dementia. Blind in his left eye, he can barely see out of his right, and on top of losing his hearing he has a hard time getting up and down. I know his days are numbered, but he has brought so much love and happiness to our home, I simply cannot imagine my life without him. Like Martin before him, Doodle simply wasn't ever meant to leave Casa Spade.

6 MIRACLE

In August, the heat can be blistering often exceeding temperatures of 100F and people stay indoors to avoiding being out in the streets. I remember I was making breakfast when I got a frantic call from Samantha to come by her office immediately. There was an emergency. I jumped in my car and headed over there knowing it must be serious.

Once I got there, there were two ladies crying, one holding a shoebox carrying a brand–less than a day–old puppy. The first few weeks of a puppy's life can be dangerous–they need their mother to survive outside the womb, to keep warm and to fend off illness and disease. In this case the mother wasn't absent but writhing from terrible pain on the examining table, the victim of a horrible accident. Two days earlier, she had been pregnant running on the streets when a neighbor witnessed her being run over by a passing car. Inconceivably the car, when running over the mama dog, killed her newborn babies as well. Running outside the neighbor discovered this and brought the badly injured mama dog inside to comfort her. At the time, they didn't realize just how bad her condition was and thought to watch overnight and bring her to the vet in the morning. Miraculously that night, she gave birth to yet another puppy and both the mom and child were wrapped in blankets and brought to Samatha first thing in the morning.

When Samantha finally examined her closely, she discovered her pelvis was broken and her bladder had exploded. She had delivered this puppy with a broken pelvis and exploded bladder! What an amazing feat for this mama. But she was in a horrible state. Samantha had performed an emergency surgery but said it was unlikely she would make it due to internal damages from the accident. Samantha placed the mom on a blanket on the floor, and I sat next to her holding her tiny puppy in my hands.

Petting the mom, I gave her hugs and kisses, letting her smell the puppy, and assuring her I'd take good care of her little baby—she needn't worry about her. The puppy was a little girl. I was in tears. Samantha was in tears. All the ladies who worked in the vet were in tears. I prayed to God asking Him to please help this poor mother if she wasn't long for this world—to at least give her the peace of mind knowing her baby would be safe in my hands. Shortly thereafter, she died.

All of us stood in silence after she passed, still in amazement of what she'd accomplished and the bravery she'd shown. It was indeed a miracle that a perfectly healthy baby could have emerged from such a tortuous ordeal. In that moment we all decided the newborn would be named Miracle in honor of her mama, and I took her home to Casa Spade full of tears but inspired by the promise I'd made to that valiant soul. I got Miracle all settled in the play yard with a new blanket and stuffed animal bottle feeding her tiny bits at a time. She was so fragile you could almost see through her fur. It wasn't hard to see when you looked at her from the start, Miracle was going to be something special.

At the time I belonged to a Facebook group in Cabo, which had a convention every year that was coming up in two weeks. I posted Miracle's story to the group in the hopes that maybe someone would want to adopt her in a couple of months. It worked. Even though she was only three weeks old when the convention had its opening dinner, when I brought her people already knew her story and asked about her. I couldn't let anyone hold her and had to keep her wrapped in a blanket the entire time, but everyone was interested in knowing "The Miracle" baby.

At that dinner, a couple that lived in California, Kathryn and Kirk, had been following her story on Facebook and expressed a real interest in adopting her. They pleaded with me to not let anyone else adopt her and even made her her own Facebook page which, within an hour, had over a hundred followers. At this point, after the convention, everyone in town knew the story of Miracle so much so that when we'd go out to dinner, people would approach us and ask to have their picture taken with the famous survivor. Miracle was a Cabo celebrity.

She continued to grow and Kathryn and Kirk kept their promise, continuing to be in contact as I'd send them almost daily pictures and videos that showed baby Miracle's progress. Incredibly, despite her traumatic entrance to the world, Miracle thrived just like a normal puppy showing no signs of her birth ordeal.

Two and a half months later Kathryn and Kirk came back to Cabo to pick up Miracle. They had not seen her in person since she was two weeks old. I had her dressed in the cutest little dress and we met them at a restaurant just outside of town. Kirk immediately took her, walked outside, sat down on the ground and began to cry. They had waited a long time for this meeting. Miracle rewarded her new daddy with kisses and then later fell asleep in Kathryn's lap while we were eating. To our great surprise, Kirk and Kathryn had decided they wanted to marry while in Cabo and asked if John and I would be their witnesses. "Of course!" We exclaimed. We were not only surprised but honored. The connection between us thanks to Miracle felt like family, and so we immediately set out to plan an intimate wedding at the private beach in our neighborhood. I was able to find someone with the authority to marry them plus a photographer, while the happy couple took care of the license and blood tests. John even picked out an adorable little fancy dress for Miracle to wear during the ceremony. A couple days later, down at Cabo Bello Beach, Kathryn and Kirk were wed with Miracle and the rest of us as their witness.

I could have never imagined Miracle's story would turn out this way after the tragic circumstances surrounding our first encounter. But despite that, now she was going to be loved and happy with her newly wedded mom and dad. When the day came to take little Miracle home, I knew it was going to be a tough one. Since the moment I made mama a life promise, I had grown attached to this little girl and I cried ugly at the airport. The only thing that comforted me was knowing she was going to such a special home with two people who truly loved her. But we did have a special bond.

Once she made it to California, Miracle loved running on the beach. She loved finding and chasing the stick while running into the crashing waves. She loved hiking the creek behind her home. John and I went to visit about two years later and Miracle stood in the front yard barking just barking at us. I kept calling her name, asking if she remembered me and when she heard my voice, suddenly she ran towards me. I was in tears yet again. Jumping on to me and licking my face, she did zoomies all around the yard. The few days we spent at Kirk and Kathryn's, Miracle would not leave my side–she even slept in bed with us. It was special not only to visit with her again but to see how happy she'd become living in California as a beach girl.

Two years ago, Kirk and Kathryn moved to Illinois. They didn't have a fenced yard, so Miracle would disappear for nearly two hours every day. Kirk decided to put a Go Pro camera on her harness just to see where she was running off to and he discovered she simply ran through the neighborhood:

41

chasing birds, playing through the stream and visiting neighbors—enjoying and relishing the miracle of life. Sadly, just recently she has been diagnosed with cancer and isn't as active as she once was. Now her favorite thing is to sit on the front porch in her doggie couch and watch the birds and squirrels. She is not in any pain as they give her medication, so she will just live out the rest of her life in beautiful Illinois surrounded by her loving parents. She will be eleven years old this year. Kathryn and Kirk still come to Cabo, and we keep in touch despite not seeing each other as often. The bond that was created by Miracle is special and everlasting—a reminder that life is not just precious but something to be cherished. I am grateful to have kept my promise.

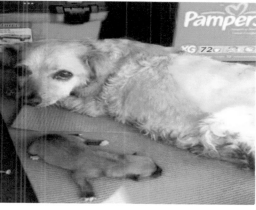

7 CHICA & SANDY

I used to walk the marina three miles very early every morning, catching the beautiful sunrise over Playa Empacadora. This beach is a beach where the local Mexicans would take their families to go swim in the ocean. It's not a tourist area. Oftentimes after my walk, I would sit by the beach, watching the sunrise and the early morning fisherman going out to their boats.

On this particular morning, I was sitting in the sand when a Mexican local walked up to me with these two fat, fluffy little puppies. She said, "you're Penny, 'The Puppy Lady', right? I was surprised that a stranger would know that but then again I had been fostering puppies for quite a few years by this time and I was notorious for being seen walking my puppies along the marina. I responded with a faint, "yes" pretty sure that she was going to want to hand me these two little puppies. They were about eight weeks old and appeared to be quite healthy. I assumed the locals had been feeding them but was baffled as to why no one had taken them home or dropped them off at the Humane Society—the fire department, a vet office—somewhere safe. Whatever the reason I knew they could not live alone on the rocks at the beach.

They were both girls and beautiful puppies, one a tan color with short hair and one a white long haired puppy. Of course I took them from this lady and immediately took them to Samantha for testing. I've said this before but it is imperative that any puppies of this age get tested before bringing them into my house because they could be contagious and need to be quarantined. Even though my dogs are older and have all their shots you still have to be careful. Fortunately, once again, they tested negative and because of their age they also got their first deworming and puppy vaccine. I hadn't fostered for a while so it was fun to have babies back in the house. Pulling out the play yard, setting it up and getting them all settled—felt like old times. I had plenty of the necessary provisions in storage as well.

They were adorable and I could tell just by how they were acting that they were so glad to be off those rocks at the beach and in a clean, comfortable home with an endless supply of food, water and love. I gave them a bath and fed them some before they both curled up on the baby blankets in the play yard and slept better than they had probably slept since they were born. It was obvious they were dumped on the rocks. Due to the location of the beach and the rocks on which they were found, there was no way they could have just appeared there on their own.

After a week of acclimation, I started taking them down to the marina with me on my morning walks, hoping to find them homes. Having the puppies in the wagon generally attracted the right kind of attention and on this particular morning I happened to pass by a restaurant where a guy I knew worked as a bartender. He came out from behind the bar to pet them and fell head over heels in love with the white fluffy one. Already having a dog at home, he thought maybe his dog could use a playmate. He asked for a couple days to think about it which was no problem given they still needed to get fixed and finish their puppy shots. "Sure thing!" I said, one puppy down just one more to go.

I'd already sent photos to my rescue partner Suzanne in Portland who owned a puppy shelter called Rescue Faerie. They'd been taking most of my puppies when they turned three months and were vaccinated and fixed. I tended to send a picture when they were close to adoption age and Suzanne would post them on Pet Finder in the hopes of finding good candidates before the puppies even got there. Oftentimes this would lead to adoptions the day they arrived in Portland.

Rescue Faerie already had taken quite a few of my foster puppies by this time and Suzanne had an amazing gift of matching the perfect puppy with the perfect owner. It just happened that someone in Portland who had adopted one of my puppies a year prior from Rescue Faerie saw the brown one on Pet Finder and said they were very interested in her which was great news. Also a week later the bartender decided that he definitely wanted to adopt the white one and he was going to name her Arena which means sand in Spanish—an appropriate name considering where she was found. When it was time to take her to her new dad I gave her a bath and got a big bow and surprised him at the end of his shift where he was working. He took one look at her and literally cried when he saw her and picked her up out of the wagon. A match made in heaven. I talk to his wife at church now and then and she told me Sandy/Arena is doing great and loves to play tug-o-war and hang out with her in the bathroom whenever she gets ready in the morning. Most of the time she is pure sweetness and camera shy but sometimes she also likes to show her fierce side now and again.

As for the brown one, the couple in Portland, Suzie and Mike had already been approved and named her Chica. They said she would be a perfect fit with her big brother, Peso who they'd found as well through Rescue Faerie the year before. This time I was fortunate enough to personally deliver Chica to Portland to Rescue Fairie and meet Suzie and Mike. I got to witness the start to finish of my foster efforts. They were so sweet, so perfect and so excited to arrive at her new home and meet her brother. Chica and Peso are doing amazing and inseparable, growing up loving each other in the beautiful countryside in Portland. Chica is a bit of a drama queen. She loves to talk and is always whining around about something. She feels deep. Her favorite thing to do is chase the ball and run. Sadly she was having too much fun and blew out both knees when she was a puppy and had to have surgeries to correct them. Now she can run again and again, loving life happily in the country. I also keep in touch with Suzie and she keeps me updated on Peso and Chica.

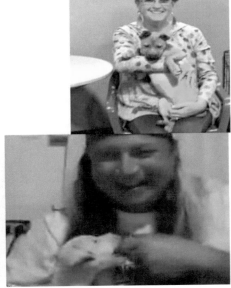

8 NICKI, JACKI, & SOPHIA

A few days after Hurricane Lidia hit and devastated Cabo, one of the worst hit areas was on the ocean side of the highway just about a half mile outside of town. The damage took out an entire car dealership and trailer park. Many cars from the dealership were swept away with the force of mud and water out into the ocean or simply flipped over on top of each other leaving the dealership, or what was left of it, a twisted pile of torn metal. The same fate met the trailer park next door. Whichever trailers and cars hadn't been washed out into the ocean were caked in mud and debris.

Amidst this wasteland, a resident of the park was walking around and assessing the damage when she stumbled upon a mama dog and her four puppies cowering in the mud under a mattress trapped underneath a broken-down trailer. A fellow rescuing colleague contacted me and asked if I could come get them. When I arrived at the trailer park, I couldn't even enter due to the mud. So I parked on the highway and carried my kennel with me, trucking through the mud until I reached the puppies. They were smothered in mud but adorable and all so happy to see me. I sat down and pet them, gave them some fresh food and water and assessed the situation.

I wasn't comfortable taking them with me at that time, because I couldn't be sure they didn't belong to anybody at the park, who might come back looking for them. Still, I couldn't leave them where they were under a mattress soaking in the wet mud. I happened upon an old wooden bed frame and put it down in an area that was mostly cement. In my kennel there was clean bedding which fit nicely in the frame along with a bag of dog food and a jug of water. Luckily the frame was tall enough that the puppies couldn't escape—at least it seemed that way. I left and returned bright and early the next morning eagerly expecting to see them all intact.

Three of the puppies were there, one was missing, but the mama dog was nowhere to be found. I called for the mama dog but she didn't come. The entire park was nothing but mud and debris and my heart ached for these missing two. Either the mom had left completely and taken one puppy with her or somebody else had come and taken just one puppy. It just wasn't possible that the puppy could have escaped on its own. I phoned a friend who also rescues to see if she could come and look for them both and immediately took the other three home with me to Casa Spade. On the way home, of course I was filled with pangs of what if–what if I'd taken them all home the night before–of course you're haunted by these thoughts. But you also know you make the best decisions you can in the heat of the moment, God forbid you take somebody's puppies who just lost their home. I left my number at the spot where I'd placed the bed frame and focussed on these three little souls who were now in my care.

The first thing I did once back safely at Casa Spade was give them baths–a not so easy task given how caked they were with mud. Out of that strenuous task came their colors which turned out to be brindle and brown. Part of my training with puppies is one word commands, sit, stay, eat, potty, bedtime. Training anything, especially puppies, is all about repetition. With these three puppies, I set up the play yard with the pee pads on one side and their blankets on the other. Puppies will not sleep where they pee unless they have no other choice. So for me, it's very important to always keep a clean play yard. I've also learned over the years if I layer the pee pads it makes things even easier to keep up with the cleaning of the play yard. Whenever they soil one, there's a clean one right underneath it. I am such a neat freak when it comes to my puppies. Boy did I go through a lot of pee pads in those fifteen years of fostering.

I would also buy huge packages of rolls of blue paper towels like you use in your garage. Those towels absorb pee very quickly and neatly once the puppies are allowed to roam around the house. Of course I would also set pee pads out by the door to get them used to and eventually go outside to pee. I would always feed puppies in the play yard. When it was time to eat I would just say the word eat and they would dash back to the open play yard door, go inside and sit so adorable in anticipation of their meal. Another thing I learned over the years is that immediately after puppies eat they pee and poop. This means that they would stay in the play yard until that deed was done. Then I could let them run around the house and interact with my dogs for some training on how to behave. It's all about repetition. Do the same thing over and over and eventually it clicks, they get it, and then they're very easy to handle.

I would take the puppies down to the marina in the wagon on my morning walks to socialize them and introduce them to the tourists. After awhile doing it, the moment my wagon was spotted coming down the marina, somebody would pop out from the tourist booths, shouting, "Here comes Penny, The Puppy Lady!" Throngs of people would stream out to pet the puppies as I walked past their booths. I trained the puppies to walk on a leash which is always a funny sight to behold: as soon as you put them on a leash they become paralyzed with fear. They plant their feet and refuse to move. Everyone at the marina got a kick out of it, taking lots and lots of pictures. Sometimes people visiting Cabo on cruise ships or simply on vacation missing their own animals back home would take comfort in seeing a friendly soul so far away. It's good therapy and a comfort—both for the tourists and the puppies, who receive so much adulation and attention.

Eventually after two months at Casa Spade the time came for these three little amazing angels to travel to Portland to their forever homes. They were joined by two other pups, but between the five of them they were too big to travel up top—they had to go in kennels down below. It was an issue. When we arrived in Portland everyone had gone home for the night and my four kennels were the last to arrive in baggage claim. Not to worry, I'd been through worse. As I loaded the kennels onto a luggage cart and tracked it across the airport to meet the shuttle, I asked myself, "Is this how you want to spend your retirement?" Of course it was. By the time I finally traversed the entire airport and switched between two shuttles I knew that if the puppies were quiet then I could carry on. They were sweet little patient soldiers. They didn't even pee until an hour later when we were waiting for Suzanne to arrive with Rescue Faerie and I spotted a grassy patch of land. We loaded up the kennels in her car and breathed a big sigh of relief: another successful rescue.

The puppies were named Nicki, Jacki and Sophia, and sadly I didn't get to find out who adopted them in the end as I returned to Cabo the next morning. I did find out the mama dog was discovered in the trailer park a day after I left and she found a home in Canada thank God. There was so much devastation in the trailer park that day, it's still mind-blowing to think this mama and her puppies could survive. I pray the other puppy survived in and is in someone's loving arms. I know that God wasn't ready to take them yet, that's the only explanation that makes sense.

9 LOLA & LALO

The story of these two, husband and wife, is probably the most unusual and interesting story I have experienced. I got a call from the Humane Society that someone had just surrendered two basset hounds about four years old. I was honestly blown away. They were adorable and beautiful. How could someone take both their pet dogs they had since they were puppies and surrender them to the Humane Society?

The answer was disturbing. The female had been bred so many times her whole stomach was dragging to the ground. Evidently the owners just kept them to make money selling their offspring. Now that they couldn't make any more money on them, they were of no use to them. Little did they know Lola was pregnant when they dropped them off at the shelter. You could not tell she was pregnant because of the dragging of her stomach. Her nipples were all dried up and crusty. They asked me if I could take Lola until she had her babies, and they were old enough to be adopted. That was a no brainer for me. Of course I was going to take her. This was a first for me because I always received puppies when they were abandoned; now I would witness an actual birth. My husband built a whelping box which was also a first for us. I researched how to do it on YouTube, and we built one that had an opening on one side so that mama could get in and out with her big, dragging belly. Mama was aggressive towards my dogs even though she was slow-moving. She didn't want to be pregnant; she didn't want to be at my house. She missed her partner, and she was scared.

On the second day, she gave birth to three adorable little puppies, a brown one and two black ones. Sadly one of the black ones was stillborn. But the other two appeared to be very healthy. It was an amazing sight to behold. There was a small problem though. Due to moms physical condition she wasn't able to nurse the puppies. I had to make bottles of formula and I would sit in the whelping box and bottle feed the puppies then put them right back with the mom. It was tricky, but it kept mama stress free and puppies fed. There were sleepless nights feeding the puppies about every two to three hours but we made it. Eventually, Lola became more comfortable in the house, and in six weeks the puppies could eat on their own. Then the whole family—Lola, Lalo, and the puppies—were driven to the Daphneyland Basset Hound Rescue in California. Someone donated money for Lola to have a tummy tuck and both were fixed. The two puppies would eventually get adopted, but Lola and Lalo were going to live out the rest of their lives at the sanctuary with other Basset Hounds. Unfortunately I was not able to keep in touch with the rescue in California but I heard they were welcomed with open arms and doing great. That was the first time I personally witnessed the birth of puppies and it was such a miracle to watch.

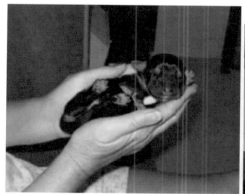

10 HITCH

Hitch, sweet, sweet little Hitch—what a rough beginning this little boy had...

One rainy night around 9:30 I was scrolling through Facebook and came across a post about a young girl who had found a puppy two days earlier just laying in the rain and mud on the street in her neighborhood out in the barrios. She had stated in her post that she picked him up and took him home but then soon realized he was more than she personally could take care of. She put a post on Facebook if anyone could help her out and please come get him.

Everyone in town already knew I would be the one to step in and take this little guy, and I immediately started getting tagged in the post as well. I messaged the girl and told her I would definitely take him and could we meet in a half hour in a grocery store parking lot close to where she lived. As planned she arrived with her dad and brought this tiny, little puppy over to my car, handing him over to me. She was in tears, because she really wanted to help and take care of him. I felt for her. She seemed to be only thirteen and had great expectations and I applaud her for that, but she did the right thing in reaching out to somebody that could—if everyone was as responsible as that little girl, there would be a lot less deceased puppies in the world.

As I've mentioned in several stories, there are so many places people can hand over unwanted puppies or kittens and they don't have to throw them in the trash or just leave them alone on the sidewalk in the rain. When she handed him to me he was much smaller than he looked in the picture. He was very malnourished and scruffy-looking. Not my first rodeo, though, and I knew I could help this little guy. I got him home and of course cleaned him up and fed him right away with some warm formula. Poor little guy was freezing and

56

starving half to death literally. He seemed to be about two weeks old. So who knew how long he had been laying there in the rain with people walking by and just ignoring him? It really upsets me to think of the indifference–it never gets any easier, only harder.

When I picked him up it was too late to take him to Samantha, so I had to just stay with him until morning. Of course as with all new puppies, there was not much sleep to be had, not necessarily because of him waking me up but because of his awful condition. You can't countenance a puppy dying because you fell asleep. It's not the mark of a hero, you're just simply engaged in saving another soul–you pray you, connect, you're there until it ends.

Happily the little guy bravely made it through the night and the next morning at Samanthas we were both surprised to discover that although he was malnourished and had clearly starved, it wasn't past the point of no return. With some TLC and time, he would catch up and put on some weight. What a relief! Back to Casa Spade we went to fill the marching orders.

I have a friend in California named Lisa who's daughter Marley has helped me name lots of my puppies. After the first fifty puppies you start running out of names. I would send her pictures and tell her their story and she would pick names for them. She thought about this little guy and said Hitch would be the perfect name. That he was trying to hitch a ride to a new home that's why he was just laying on in the street. Made sense and was sweet, so from then on he was called Hitch. Once Hitch got to a normal weight, his coat started coming in and he was a beautiful black and white puppy. He was a great puppy but as I'd mentioned before, often times when puppies are abandoned they can develop behavioral issues.

Hitch started showing a nipping behavior. Not a hard bite but a nipping one that was probably due to him not having his mom or siblings in the yard to play with and teach him boundaries. He was nipping at the other dogs in the house or anyone who would come up to him, even me! But as I'm not a dog trainer, I didn't know how to fix the situation. It was my first puppy with this issue and I was at a loss for what to do.

Thankfully, Samantha put me in touch with a dog trainer who specialized in these sorts of problems. He took Hitch to live with him for fifteen days. As it was explained to me the trick to get rid of nipping is to gently hold him down with one hand behind his neck until he became submissive and gave in. That's what the mom would do with her paw if she were around. Once Hitch returned, the nipping was a lot better but didn't completely go away. It was certainly good enough to send his pictures to Suzanne at Rescue Faerie and once he had all his puppy shots and was fixed, Hitch was ready to find his new family.

Hitch was adopted immediately by a family Patrice and Mike who had a little ten year old boy named Max that they'd adopted as a baby. One thing I began doing with the single puppies is keep a little journal with their pictures and story to give to their new family. Hitch had such a journal. When Max received Hitch's journal, he was so excited he took the story book to school for show and tell. He regaled his classmates and teacher with pictures of where Hitch was found in the dirt, how he used to walk on a leash at the marina and swim in the pool. Max was a very proud big brother.

Once Patrice reached out to me and said the nipping behavior had returned. I warned them about it at first but hoped it would go away on its own. Using the same technique I'd been taught, Patrice actually wrestled Hitch to the ground until he learned who was the boss. He came with so much energy sometimes he just didn't know what to do with it. But eventually by asserting dominance, Patrice was able to tame the wild beast within and now Hitch treats her like his pack leader never leaving her side. He follows her everywhere at all times. Hitch even sleeps with Patrice and her husband Mike.

Sadly, Hitch isn't fond of other dogs and even barks excitedly at them on the television but he does love people. He loves the UPS driver who invites him in his truck and always gives him treats. He lives on two acres of land with plenty of room to explore, exercise, camp and chase the waves on the beach. Hitch is a team player always accompanying the family while they're doing yardwork, planting flowers and burning yard debris. Still a Cabo dog as he hates the rain, but he loves the country where he lives. He loves chasing squirrels, bunnies, and deer who roam the property and is a fantastic watchdog that looks after Max who's become his best friend as they run around the property.

Max and his little brother play tug of war with Hitch's favorite rope toy and they chase each other around the house playing keep away. Although not a snuggly dog, Hitch does allow Max to lay down on the floor to snuggle as much as he allows. Patrice, Mike and Max all love Hitch being part of their family and couldn't imagine life without him.

me.

11 FIVE RANDOM PUPPIES

In my early, early days of fostering other than my vet Samantha, I didn't have the experience I would receive later with what puppies needed other than food, water, a clean area for them to roam and lots of love and affection. I didn't have the connections I got later as to where to send puppies once they were vaccinated and fixed and ready for adoption. I was still a newbie to the fostering world. I did take my dogs, Marlin and Vicente, to doggy daycare every Thursday. I didn't have Doodle yet during this time. On one Thursday, as I dropped my dogs off for the day, the owner said he needed help with something. I had no idea what he could possibly need help with because he was also a dog trainer. He took me back to his office and said when they came to open that morning someone during the night had dropped off five puppies in a box. These puppies were already about ten weeks old, eating on their own, looked healthy, fat and fluffy, and each was a different color. He asked if I could please take them and find them good homes. It was summer. It was hot. We didn't have air conditioning at the time. We also didn't have our pool up and running. But they pulled at my heart strings with those little puppy dog eyes when I looked at them in the box. It made me think of Katy when she found Marlin, Sassy and Lucy in a box on her front gate. If I didn't take them, who would take them?

I had to give them a chance. What the heck, I loaded them up in my car anyway and said I'd do what I could. This was before the days of play yards or pee pads. This was the early days. I had maybe fostered three or four single puppies since Marlin, Sassy and Lucy before I brought these five homes. I took them to Samantha. God what would I have done without Samantha? She was my Puppy Goddess. I depended on her probably way more than I should have. But I totally trusted her. She was and still is an amazing vet and always seems to know exactly what to do. She has been a life saver over my fifteen years of fostering.

I've always been pleasantly surprised at how healthy my puppies have been relatively speaking. Samantha does her tests and most often they come back negative. All puppies have worms, for example, and it's very easy to get rid of with medication. But I can't recall a single puppy that ever had a major disease—maybe that's the magic of Samantha. So these five puppies received their tests, came back negative and I brought them back to the house. Now I didn't have the play yard set up at this point, so I sent John to Home Depot to get some chicken wire and we screened off our front porch for the newborns.

Being new to town, I just started advertising through friends and social media to see if anyone was interested in adopting. To my surprise, within two weeks all five were not only vaccinated and fixed but adopted locally. One went to a realtor, one to a single guy, two went to my best friend Pepita and her husband Ron, and the other one went to a family with small children. It was a quick intake, but I was fortunate enough to find them all great homes. Pepita and Ron named theirs Lola and Sara. Sadly, Sara passed away two years ago. Lola's still around. I think of these five puppies as the first time I knew this would be my life, my new normal. It's one thing to raise a single puppy, but five, that's a commitment. Looking back at those five random puppies showed me this was who I was going to be.

12 BEN & JERRY

One morning a local realtor friend went to her car to head to work when she noticed next to her driveway something was moving in a small plastic bag. She opened the bag and inside, to her astonishment, were two puppies squirming and crying. They looked to be about a week old, and her guess was that someone had left them there hoping she'd discover them when she started her car. Their eyes hadn't even opened yet, so their world was still dark.

She called me straight away, and I told her to bring them to her office where I swing by to pick them up. She was in tears. "How can people just dump these little babies?" She asked. I told her that some people just don't care. The gift was that at least the babies were left where they could be found and weren't buried in the trash as often happens. "It's still heartbreaking but they have a chance now that you've found them."

When I picked up the babies, I took them to Samantha for tests, and she assured me they'd be fine–it seemed like I needed the Puppy Goddess' seal of approval for all my puppies. At this point, I had fostered quite a few, so I was comfortable these little boys would be fine, but Samantha's consent always helped me begin my work.

Since they were still only a week old they couldn't receive any kind of treatment, so I brought them home and put them in a kennel with a heating pad in the bottom and a blanket on top rather than the play yard. I fed them as they were starving and was able to observe their colors more closely. One was brown and the other black. They were so adorable which is what I say about all puppies, but honestly who's ever seen an ugly puppy? I called Marley, my puppy-namer, and sent her pictures to which she whipped up the names, Ben and Jerry. She never explained why: I think inspiration hit her in mysterious ways.

In the second week, Ben got really sick, and was having trouble breathing. I took him to Samantha and she put him on oxygen. He was so tiny that his whole head fit inside the plastic oxygen mask. I stayed with him for a few hours holding the oxygen mask over his tiny face while he lay on the exam table. Little by little, it seemed like he was getting better. Smantha released him later that day but said to keep a close eye on him. This would turn out to be an interesting turn of phrase as two weeks later, I noticed his right eyelid looked strange. It seemed to have flipped upwards and exposed the entire inside of his pinkish upper eyelid. I'd never seen anything like that before, so back to Samantha we went.

My hunch was correct: it was indeed a flipped eyelid, but the remedy to fix it was something out of a spy novel. After a light sedation, Samantha sewed a button on his eyelid to keep it straight–yes a button. Henceforth, he would be renamed Benjamin Buttons and required to keep the button on for several weeks. His condition required he be kept separate in the play yard, which was fine, so that none of the other pups would inadvertently rip off this precious button.

This all took place before I'd encountered Rescue Faerie, so I'd been advertising photos of Ben (Button) and Jerry on Facebook. A friend's sister and her husband, Dianna and Tom, reached out and said they were very interested in adopting them. They lived close by, so I took both pups over to meet them and they fell in love at first sight confirming yes they wanted to adopt them both. They still needed their vaccinations and to get fixed, but this was perfect as it gave Tom time to build a beautiful wooden and wire play yard to greet them on their arrival.

Finally the day came for them to go to their 4ever home. Dianna and Tom were so excited to welcome these two little boys into their beautiful home with a gorgeous ocean view. They were two very lucky puppies. Today Jerry weighs eight pounds more than Ben. Ben has hip dysplasia so he is not as active as Jerry and seems to always have some kind of skin issue. They've had him on many different medications for ear mites and dry patches on his fur–sadly one of the many issues with abandoned puppies never knowing from where they came nor what condition their mama was in when she gave birth. Dianne says that Ben had been very aggressive since he was a puppy, but now he is a very loving dog. Both Ben and Jerry are excellent watch dogs and keep them informed whenever a horse runs by. Jerry, for his part, is a real ladies man, always preening for attention and once gotten, begs for more. He also had a fetish for dog beds and has chewed up quite a few over the years. Ben likes to sleep on a carpet and never leaves Tom's side. They couldn't have asked for two better companions.

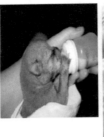

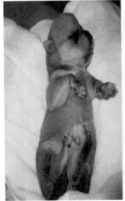

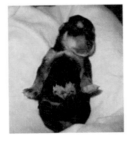

13 DUKE

So many of these stories begin sounding like a broken record with puppies thrown away as trash, but that's the reality of abandoned puppies. Being thrown in a dumpster is the norm. Hence we arrive at the story of Sir Duke Ellington, another dumpster puppy who defied the odds.

I received a call from my niece, Gina, who lives in Cabo, that a vet in San Jose del Cabo had just received a small, gray puppy that someone had just brought in that was discarded in a dumpster. The rescue she worked with was full and asked if I would take him. From the picture she sent he looked to be about two months old. He was beautifully gray with some distinct pit bull in him. I set up Casa Spade for the arrival of our new foster. Whenever I begin to set up, my dogs instinctively know a new baby is soon to arrive. They seem to have a sixth stork sense like birds flying south for the winter. What they didn't know—what they couldn't have known—as I didn't either, was that Sir Duke would be one last of my foster puppies.

When I arrived at the vet, he was much smaller than what I'd expected from his picture; worse still, he was shaking, scared and had the saddest look on his tiny face. I've said it often in these pages, but it just breaks your heart to see an abandoned puppy. It never gets easier despite the number you've seen: the same sad eyes, the same scared look on their faces. There's a universal look to being helpless and vulnerable that each one of them carries—that's the hard part. But when you take them out of the kennel for the first time, when I held Duke who simply melted in my arms—that feeling of love, that feeling of belonging—that too never goes away and gives you the strength to keep coming back. I fell in love immediately and knew I needed to get this little guy home where he felt safe.

He seemed to settle down pretty quickly once he ate and discovered he had a clean, soft area to play with toys and plenty of food and water. He didn't have to be alone anymore. Of course the other dogs had to greet him and smell him as they're wont to do. I just let him settle in the play yard for a bit and get comfortable. He took a nice, long nap and snuggled up to a little teddy bear. Even though I picked him up from one vet, Sir Duke still needed a trip to the Puppy Goddess and get a clean bill of health. The next morning I took him to see Samantha who likewise couldn't believe how tiny he was compared to his photo. He weighed in at four pounds, nineteen ounces, and had all his tests which, thanks to Samantha's lucky charm, came back free and clear.

He turned out, as expected, to be around two months old and was simply small for his age. He got his first vaccination and deworming and while he was in good shape, he did have a skin issue we'd hoped was due to his diet or lack thereof. The skin issue required a good rub down with coconut oil and wearing a onesie that turned out to complement his personality. John had a habit of always giving the puppies a bite of his food when he was finished and Duke was no different. He would wait patiently, along with the rest of the dogs, except he was wearing a onesie which gave him a competitive advantage–an unfair advantage, but it worked all the same. He was a natural under the table. Sir Duke also, as it turned out, didn't like to be confined to the play yard. Within a few days he figured out his escape and found his way up the stairs to my bed. For as long as he was a resident at Casa Spade, that's where he slept–a world-class snuggler tucked right under my chin. He was also a true sport on the wagon or in the puppy sling and loved his trips to the marina where he received no shortage of attention from the people passing by. As he arrived in December when the weather was cool, he threw on an extra layer of t-shirts that only made him look even more dang cute.

Upon his second vet visit, Sir Duke had gained three pounds in one week, so it was time to think of his adoption. After six weeks of living at Casa Spade I got a call from my friend Erica, a huge dog rescuer in Cabo that had made some calls to her connections living in California. One of those friends, Danyelle, a singer, was very interested in adopting Sir Duke, and Erica offered to escort him on his trip to California. By this time he was already vaccinated and fixed, leash trained, house broken, socialized and ready to travel. Whenever a puppy travels it has to get a letter from the vet saying that it has been vaccinated and has no existing health issues and is given a health/travel certificate along with his vaccination booklet.

The day before many of my puppies leave they have a spa day with groomer

Daniel who owns Pelu Dogs Grooming. He is an amazing groomer in Cabo, who's groomed all my babies for sixteen years and is amazingly gentle with the puppies. After he's finished, he always puts a cute little bandana around their necks, and if a girl, a pretty pink bow in their hair. Duke was one of those lucky puppies who knew exactly how handsome he was when he emerged with his silver shiny coat and devilish grin worn ear to ear.

On the morning he was set to travel, I loaded up Sir Duke in the kennel and went to grab Erica at the Humane Society. She was escorting a few more puppies on their behalf. I dropped them all off at the airport drop, parked the car and walked inside to meet with them. I am proud to say that I personally have never had a puppy that couldn't travel, but one time I was dropping off friends at the airport and saw a lady with a kennel looking frantic. I stopped and asked her if there was a problem. She said the airline wouldn't allow her dog to fly because he was too big for the kennel she'd brought. Imagine that? She was waiting for someone to come pick up the dog and would miss her flight. Luckily I convinced her to board and offered to deliver the dog to the friend's home. For that reason I never leave an escort until both they and the dog are successfully checked in. And this was the case with Sir Duke— everything went as planned. I waved goodbye with tears forming in my eyes wishing him the best in his new life, his new 4ever home with Danyelle in California.

It turns out Duke loves his new home. He got to experience snow shortly after arriving in California. I've kept in touch with Danyelle since the adoption and she says Sir Duke loves the pool or anything else filled with water. I had a hunch he'd turn out to be a water dog. He loves being out on their boat and cruising around the lake. He is a good, smart and handsome boy who definitely has a temper. He can not sleep without a blanket and he loves to cuddle with his mama. I wonder where he got that from? He's very protective of his family and anytime his sisters need to go outside to use the restroom, he will accompany them. He's always there by their side watching over them. Duke now weighs a whopping seventy pounds! I knew he was going to be big, but that's a big dog. Danyelle sends me pictures now and then and he is still as handsome as the day he walked out of Pely's groomers...he's only missing his onesie.

14 CAM & SUNNY

One of my partner rescuers, Mariana, owns Dog Prana that takes in mostly pregnant moms and keeps both mama and the puppies until they vaxxed and fixed. She then finds 4ever homes for them. She has an amazing track record and runs a tremendous operation funded only on donations and with her daughter, Ema, and few volunteers.

I got a call from Mariana that someone had dropped off two brand new puppies whose mom had unfortunately passed away. Without their mom, these two little puppies, a boy and girl, needed to be bottle-fed and she didn't feel comfortable doing it on her own. She called me and asked if I wouldn't mind taking them off her hands. Of course I would take them. I made the hour drive to Pescadero to meet these precious souls that had the sweetest "take care of me" look, it made you melt. They were about two weeks old, eyes still closed. Since the majority of my rescue puppies were newborns I had no problem bringing them home. One, the boy, we named Cam, and he was solid brown. The other was a girl, we named Sunny, and she had long, white hair. They were beyond adorable. I put them in the kennel in my car and they both screamed the entire hour ride home–not so adorable.

I was trying to play the radio, sing to them, talk to them, put my hand in their kennel to pet them, but they just wanted to eat. When puppies set their mind to cry they will cry and cry, and cry until you feed them. I'd hoped the car ride would put them to sleep, but I was wrong–not these little babies. After what felt like an eternity, we finally made it home, and I was able to feed them after which they promptly passed out, and I quickly followed from exhaustion.

At the time we had a male friend named Mike who had Parkinsons and Dementia living with us. I was his full-time caregiver. He had been with us for a year when I brought the puppies home. Yes, along with taking care of puppies I also take care of humans on occasion. I took care of his wife, Judi, two years prior when she had stomach cancer until she sadly passed. Mike stayed in his room most of the time, and so I took note when he kept looking fondly at the puppies as I bottle fed them. As I finished, I asked if he wanted to hold them and he said he did. Placing them gently in his arms, I watched as he slowly rocked them to sleep smiling as he did. I think it gave him peace to see these beautiful creatures so peaceful in his lap. The next day, I peered again into his room again after I'd begun to feed and there he was looking gently out at us. We continued to process every day, sometimes twice for six weeks. The puppies gave a very small but important meaning to his day and he, in return, was a source of comfort and stability as they continued to grow.

As they grew bigger, a friend contacted me saying she knew someone looking to get a puppy for their two daughters who were very active and needed a dog to accompany them on their hiking and camping trips. We picked a day to meet and I took Cam and Sunny over to their house to play with the girls. They hit it off with Sunny immediately and after a couple more play dates the girls had convinced their father to let Sunny join the family. By this time he was vaxxed and fixed, I went to the store and bought a big pink bow to tie around her neck. It's a bit of a tradition for me, I like sending them off the best I can. I bought a couple cute toys and placed Sunny inside a wicker basket wrapped in her new blanket. When I drove to their house and knocked on the door, I set the basket down to the ground and moved to the side so they couldn't see me. The two girls opened the door and screamed wild with excitement—their new hiking companion had arrived. As you can imagine, these little moments are what makes everything worth it.

After the excitement died down a bit, I sat with the girls and explained their new responsibilities. They needed to make sure he had access to water both inside and out plus they needed to feed him twice a day. Agreeing on the spot, the girls also promised to love her and pet her and hug her so she felt part of the family. It was darling. The entire family was present to witness the agreement. Since then, I've learned Sunny has grown into a beautiful, long white haired dog that goes hiking every morning with the girls and their dad in the mountains behind their house. Sunny sleeps with the girls and also joins them at the beach to which they go often. She has been a great addition to the family and is absolutely loved by all.

Now what to do with Cam. Cam was a water dog who loved the pool. As soon the door opened, he was the first to scurry past and jump in the pool. Bypassing the stops he dove straight to the bottom to retrieve toys. Cam was also a very stocky boy, very strong and muscular. Given the connection he already had with Mike, it seemed Cam might make an excellent service dog. It was a very tough decision as Vincene had passed a year earlier and Marlin was getting older. Both Mike and John were so close to Cam, but his love for the water presented complications I couldn't overlook. Having tile floors throughout the house, after he'd swim he'd run inside carrying the water inside with him and creating a falling hazard for both Mike and John. Moreover, I knew Cam needed to be in a home that gave him regular access to water and the great outdoors. He wasn't meant to be cooped up, he needed to run.

So I made the call to Suzanne at Rescue Fairie and told her Cam needed to come to Portland to be with an active family. She agreed and began searching for a suitable match when I delivered Cam personally to her in Portland a few weeks later. Rescue Faerie had already posted him on Pet Finder and located a young, married, outdoorsy couple that kayaked, hiked in the mountains, in the snow, and also camped. It was a perfect fit. Not long after they adopted him I received a picture of Cam summiting a snow covered mountain and another kayaking in the lake. He looked to be a happy dog at home in his element. They changed his name to Spike and set him up with an Instagram page of which I am an active follower. In every picture Spike is in a lake, in the snow, eating an ice cream cone or hiking. He hit the lottery having been adopted by this wonderful couple sure to live out a long and happy life with them.

15 WINSTON, OLIVIA, DANNY, & LOUIS

These four little puppies, and I do mean little, also came from Mariana at Dog Prana. Normally I do not like to take puppies away from their moms until they're good and weaned, but I do make exceptions under survival circumstances. In this case, the puppies were chi pugs which are tiny chihuahua puppies mixed with a small pug. When I got to Dog Prana, I saw that the chi pugs looked to be about six weeks old. They were part of a litter of nine but one died at birth. Mom had done an amazing job nursing all eight pups, but she was tired and had stopped feeding them. Mariana asked if I could help and take a couple, which I thought meant two. When I saw how tiny they were and the distressed condition of the mama, it seemed only right to take the four biggest ones, which altogether didn't weigh more than a pound each. I had fostered many, many puppies by this time, and these were surely the smallest.

I brought them home and put them in the play yard. I could barely find them buried underneath the toys and blankets. These puppies were towards the end of my fostering days, and I had never seen such well-behaved, smart, funny puppies in all my previous fosters. They had the best temperament. At first, they did not like the play yard, but because they were so tiny they had no choice. They learned very quickly what the pee pads were for. I would let them out to run around my room and then I would open the play yard door and call them, and they would all just go right back in with no problem. They never really complained. They were very quiet and slept through the night in the play yard. I had several friends with kids come over to play with them and they loved to play. They didn't bite or chew and loved to snuggle and give kisses. They especially loved to climb on Marlin and sleep in his fur. If he minded, he didn't show it. Marlin was always such a good boy with babies. They were so cute trying to go up the steps to my bed. They were getting older, just not much bigger.

When it was time to visit Samantha, I put them in the wagon and wheeled them over to her office. Since they were so small and there were four of them, I didn't take them out of the house much except to see Samantha and get their vaccines. I took them to a spay and neuter clinic to get them fixed. But other than that, they were strictly confined to Casa Spade. I was afraid, their being so small, that someone might try and take one if I took them in the wagon to the marina. I only had them for a month before they went back to Mariana at Dog Prana and who found homes for them all. I never intended to do more than help Mariana and the mama out, but as I was winding down my fostering operation at the time it was such a joy to have them in the house—if only for a short while. They were the best-behaved little chi-pups, and all ended up getting adopted to amazing families.

16 HONEY

Honey was a stray picked up off the street, scared to death of her own shadow. When I received the call, it was another rescue organization asking if I could foster her for a few months just to get her socialized while they searched for a new home for her in Canada. They estimated she was around two years old.

When I got to the office I could tell this dog was indeed scared to death. She had probably been running the streets her entire life with no human contact, poor soul. With a collar and leash, I walked her to the truck with no problem, but when I went to pick her up she began to scream. It was a hot day, so the windows were down when we arrived at a stop light and she tried to escape through the window. Fortunately I grabbed the leash just in time, but it was worrisome. She wouldn't sit in my lap. When I tried to pet her, she just pulled away and cowered on the floor. This was something new. With all my new puppies their issues were inherited but not ingrained.

Honey was a different breed. I mentioned it to Samantha and she asked to bring her in so she could take a look. She suggested some X Rays and an ultrasound to rule out any broken bones or inflammation. All came back negative. She was just a scared little girl. It broke the heart. Samantha thought it best to socialize her but that seemed impossible given the short time frame I'd been given. Two months was nothing. I couldn't imagine giving her to a family in this condition. I told them that we would just keep her until she wasn't so scared.

Six months later she still cried if you tried to pick her up, but she was making other progress. She jumped up on the couch and would sit in your lap if it was on her terms. She was house broken but hated the pool. She seemed to get along great with my dogs and the puppies that came through the house. After a year, yes, we ended up keeping her for a year, I told the vets office that we were just going to adopt her. I didn't have the heart to send her to another family and traumatize her all over again when it had taken so long for her to get comfortable at Casa Spade.

So Honey became a permanent resident of Casa Spade five years ago and she has been such a welcomed little girl. She and Buster love each other so much. She still cries when you pick her up, but we do it anyway. Daniel, the groomer, said we're treating her as if she's glass. We probably were. When she goes to get groomed he picks her right up and she doesn't make a peep, little stinker. Honey loves car rides and treats from John. She lights up the room with her little smile and perky ears. We are glad we decided to keep her after all and make her a part of Casa Spade.

17 BUSTER

Dog Prana had a mama dog dropped off one afternoon that was super, super pregnant and was going to have puppies any day. She was found wandering along the side of the road and someone picked her up knowing Dog Prana took in pregnant moms. This dog was so huge she looked like a goat getting ready to give birth. She didn't even look like a dog from behind.

That afternoon she went into labor and started having puppies. When Mariana went to bed at ten o'clock, she had delivered ten puppies already. By the time Mariana got up the next morning this amazing mama dog had delivered seventeen healthy puppies. The world record for a single birth is twenty-four. She was second in line for the most puppies birthed by one mom at a single time. Mariana was overwhelmed and asked for my help.

Mom only had ten nipples and could not nurse seventeen puppies for six weeks without intervention. As the puppy lady specializing in newborns, I jumped into action. I put together numbered charts for six weeks and bought several cans of formula, bottles, shop towels and pee pads from Costco to prepare for battle. I loaded up the car with several Sharpies and masking tape and began the hour-long trip to Pescadero. The first thing we did was put a piece of masking tape on each puppy numbering one to seventeen. The mama dog wouldn't let anyone near the puppies save Mariana and her daughter, so we had to construct a wire kennel in their pen. That allowed us to take the puppies out and bottle feed them without worrying the mama dog.

First, I made several bottles of premixed baby formula. Next with one yellow shop towel we took one puppy at a time and began to feed, making sure all the information was recorded properly in the charts: one mark for each puppy next to their corresponding number. It might seem overkill, but trust me, keeping track of seventeen puppies is not easy. There's no way to know which puppy is feeding from the mama, it happens so quickly, and some invariably aren't fed.

So our job is to supplement and make sure nobody's missing out. With one volunteer helping us, it took about an hour to feed all seventeen, and this process repeated itself every four hours.

Since I was an hour away from home, instead of driving back and forth I would hang out at Dog Prana until it was time for the next feeding. Next to the mama dog, which they named Jewels, was another pen with six chiweenies, another breed I'd never fostered before. Chiweenies are a cross between chihuahuas and dachshunds, the little guys that look like hot-dog wieners. These chiweenies were already eight weeks old and were still on-sight because they needed to be vaccinated and fixed before adoption. After feeding the seventeen, I would go rest in the pen, playing with these puppies until it was time for the next round. One of the chiweenie puppies stood out to me. While his brothers and sisters just jumped on me and played with my toes, he just wanted to be held. He was brown with a white face and white belly. He'd sit on my lap for hours and fall asleep.

For several weeks we followed this same routine—feeding, playing, both he and I sleeping in each other's arms. I couldn't stop thinking about him. I wanted him so badly, but the last thing we needed in our house at that moment was another dog. Marlin had passed away. Vincente had passed away. We had Doodle and Honey, and that was enough.

Two friends of mine, Carolyn and Joe, came to visit from Texas. I had so many activities planned while they were in town, one of which was visiting the Hotel California in Todos Santos. On the way to Todos Santos I asked them if they wanted to take a detour and stop by to see the amazing seventeen puppies. Of course they did, they were thrilled. When we arrived, seeing all the puppies together blew their minds—every one was so different. They fell in love with a little girl who had a heart on her chest. Then took them to see the chiweenies. My favorite immediately came running over, and when I picked him up he started smothering me with kisses. In that moment, I made a snap decision. He belonged with me. I could feel it in my heart. I told Mariana I was taking him to his 4ever home. Surprised, she didn't understand. "Who was adopting him?" she asked.

"I was," I replied. Everyone was in shock. They looked at me confused.

"I've been praying about it," I said, "and I want to take him home to Casa Spade to be part of our family."

Mariana started crying, Joe and Carolyn cried, we all cried. Mariana went to get a little sweater and satchel since I didn't bring my puppy sling. I looked at him once more and named him Buster. Puppy number two hundred, Buster, was coming home to Casa Spade. He slept on Joe and Carolyn's lap the whole time during the car ride home and was a wonderful little boy.

I didn't know it at the time, but Buster saved me. I'd been fostering puppies for fifteen years and mentally I was drained. I was a mess. Recently, Mike, our friend with dementia, who'd been living with us passed away. Caregiving for puppies has similarities but it's not the same as taking care of mentally and physically sick human being. I was drained–mentally, physically, but most especially, emotionally. Buster was something my heart and soul desperately needed. He has been by my side for every single minute of every single day for over a year now. He rides in the car in his little seat next to me. He's in my lap when the going gets tough, and I need a friend. He's very smart, giving me lots of kisses to cheer me up. He sleeps next to me in the bed every night. If I'm on the couch or sitting in the recliner, he's right there by my side. He is my buddy. It's not as though he's more special than my other dogs. Honey doesn't like to be held, and Doodle has canine dementia, so he's in his own little world. I needed someone to take care of me, and Buster simply filled that hole in my heart.

Buster and Honey are the best of friends. They run and play and Buster always cleans Honey's eyes. Doodle's health is declining, and I know he'll soon be crossing over the Rainbow Bridge. When he does, I don't want Honey to be alone. So Buster is a solution for many problems and the last of my many fosters.

84

18 FAITH

I have written about my favorite, most memorable puppy stories, but I have one more to tell. We have a cat that if she could tell stories she'd add another hundred pages to this book. She's twelve years old. I got her and her three siblings from a girlfriend, who was playing cards one day when they kept hearing these kittens crying somewhere nearby. They didn't know where, but the crying was incessant. Finally, it was too much, and they got up from table trying to ascertain where this noise was coming from.

They found a little nest of kittens, still with their umbilical cords attached, laying in the dirt under the bushes. It was clear their mother was nowhere to be found as they'd been crying for hours. My friend called me and asked if I would take them.

"Kittens?" I thought to myself. "I've never had kittens before, I'm not even a cat person."

But while on the phone, I could hear the kittens crying in the background, and you can't turn that instinct down. "Bring them over," I told her.

She pulled up at my house, and I went out to meet her. I remember she was wearing an upside-down baseball cap. Inside were these little kittens that actually more resembled mice. I told her I couldn't guarantee anything as they were just newborns, but I'd try to do my best. I had no experience taking care of kittens, but I figured it couldn't be much different than puppies. I was wrong.

These little things were about as long as my thumb, maybe a bit bigger. I had an empty aquarium, so I put a heating pad in the bottom with a baby blanket on top. I prepared some formula in a little glass with an eye-dropper I found in the dresser. There was just no way these tiny kitten's mouths could fit around a nipple, so I hoped this would work. I picked them up one by one—all four were girls–and began trying to feed them. I couldn't tell whether it was arriving in their bellies or not. With puppies you can hear and see them swallow. These kittens were solid black, again about the size of my thumb, and smaller than anything I had ever seen.

I was worried. I tried tirelessly to get them to eat, but they didn't seem to be drinking anything. Their movements were slowed. I prayed to God asking His will to be done. If He wanted these kittens to survive, I was going to need more than my lack of experience to help them. I named them Grace, Glory, Mercy and Faith. Grace died shortly thereafter. To be honest even though I'd given them names it was impossible to know which was which. She was only four, five hours old at the most. Within a couple more hours the second one passed and then the third. I thought I was doomed. But one little girl held on, the one whose name I'd given Faith. She was a fighter. Every few hours she drank from the eye dropper even if it was just a few drops. You could feel she wanted to live.

It was close to morning now and I'd been up all night. When John awoke he buried the other three. But by the sunrise it was clear to me at least that Faith was going to make it. With each day she got bigger and bigger until we finally graduated her feeding to a tiny little bottle. Then, she drank from a bigger bottle until eventually she drank out of a dish. While I never planned on keeping her, the dogs didn't seem to mind, and she was growing cuter by the day. Plus the fact that she survived and showed the miracle of faith, she had earned herself a spot in Casa Spade. So I bought a nice cat house that looked more like a big bird cage. Tall and black with a door in the front and tiny levels with pillows attached for her to lie on. She lived there for months.

When it was time, I brought Faith to Samantha who also loves cats and she did a full battery of tests. Faith was in great shape, and I was encouraged to keep up the good work. At the house now the dogs were starting to warm to her, and she would curl up in Marlin's fur and fall asleep as all the puppies did. I set her birdcage outside, so she could receive the fresh air and meet the birds in the trees. Then I got a long leash, attached it to her cage and let her roam the patio and eventually the yard. Not knowing the instincts of cats, I wasn't sure what would happen if I let her off the leash. But I was told she wouldn't stray too far from where food is, so I gave it a shot. It worked. She wandered the yard but never left it, always returning to her cage at night to eat and use the litter box I'd attached to the bottom. At night I'd bring her cage inside and she'd sleep with the puppies.

Faith grew up with tons of puppies, playing with them and swatting them back when they got rough.   In the afternoons, she'd curl up and sleep with the newborns in the play yard. Today Faith's hair is turning gray. She sleeps more and moves slower than before. But every night she still comes inside and sleeps where she chooses, having achieved senior status in Casa Spade. During the day she still remains outside taking naps in the shade on the patio. I never once thought I might enjoy having a cat in the house, but Faith is a special treat. Especially when she brings me prizes like birds, little squirrels and iguanas as big as her. Even then, I still love her.

EPILOGUE

When I think back upon my journey as a foster mom for puppies, I'm inspired most by what it taught me. I learned to wear many different hats at once. I learned I can survive under stressful situations. I learned not to panic over every little thing—most messes can be cleaned up one step at a time. But most of all I learned what it takes to keep a fragile newborn puppy from failing—I learned how to keep it alive.

From the dumpsters to the mud-washed hurricanes to the injured pregnant mama limping forward in the sweltering summer heat, one can be forgiven to think of these poor abandoned souls as victims—as cast-aside trash to be pitied. But when you've been as close to them as I have, when you've looked in their eyes as they cling to life, reaching for the bottle and refusing to let death take them, you see them only as profiles in courage. Nothing in them speaks to being a victim.

In this sense it was they who inspired me—through their dedication, resilience and faith—they inspired me to dig deepest and match their bravery with as much compassion and commitment I could muster. Through that, I learned that I am happy and most useful caring for others—putting the welfare of others first—that's what fills my life with joy. It gives me purpose. And all the sacrifices—the sleepless nights, the endless mess, the aching heart—it's all been more than compensated by the fulfilled existence these heroic puppies have given me. I am so proud that these fragile souls not only survived but thrived in my care. I'm so thankful to Samantha and the many others who joined me in this rescuing odyssey ensuring these puppies in their short time, if it were to be short, on this planet would be met with unwavering and unconditional love. And of course I'm immensely grateful for the 4ever families who stepped up and gave these cast-aside souls an off-ramp out of loneliness and danger—4ever homes of love and safety. Nothing that I have achieved along this journey would last if not for the image of the pink bow on the puppy arriving home for the first time into the loving arms of her new family.

My journey has not just been about fostering puppies, and one kitten, it's about building connections, fostering hope and spreading universal love one wagging tail at a time. My sincerest hope is that my stories serve as a reminder that even in the face of adversity, kindness and compassion have always and still can light the way forward.

Will I ever foster again? Never say never as Samantha kindly reminds me with a photo of the last wagon of puppies, I promised five years ago would be my last. But after fifteen years and two hundred puppies, I do believe this book is my final act in fostering. Writing this book, I think, is my last chapter, and in so doing, I have learned that I am most happy and useful caring for others. It has given me a purpose; it's given my life greater meaning. And all the sacrifices—the sleepless nights, the endless mess, the aching heart from loss—all of that has been more than compensated by leading a fulfilled existence. My greatest hope now is that I can continue that journey providing for and taking care of my husband John and my five grandchildren for whom this book is written.

ACKNOWLEDGEMENTS

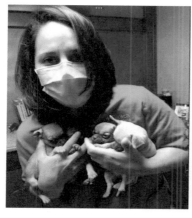

Samantha Acosta Simpero from Animal Care Clinic. Samantha has always wanted to work with animals since she was a small child. Her father was the first medical doctor to practice in Cabo. Samantha didn't want to be a medical doctor but a veterinarian. When she was six years old she went to a vet office on a field trip with her class and she saw a small surgery being performed and she was hooked. She went to Veterinarian School in Monterrey Mexico. Samantha opened her own office in Cabo twenty four years ago and is a very well respected vet in Cabo. She has been my vet ever since we got Vicente. She has seen all two hundred of my puppies over the fifteen years I have been fostering and I honestly have learned so much from her. She has been a huge part of my fostering journey. You can follow Samantha on her FB page Animal Care Center in Cabo.

Suzanne and Tom Fountain from Rescue Faerie in Portland, Oregon. Their goal is to rescue homeless dogs and cats from Mexico and find them 4ever homes in the Portland area. They work directly with them rescue organizations in Cabo and most of the dogs they work with are smaller dogs under 40 lbs. There are people in the northwest area who want smaller dogs and don't want designer dogs. They's when Rescue Faerie comes into play. There are many volunteers flying to the Portland area who are happy to escort the dogs. If none are available Tom would fly down himself and pick up the dogs. They are then taken to Lexi Dog Daycare for intake. Lexi Daycare is also run by Suzanne and Tom. They have many volunteers that walk and feed the dogs. When I had puppies I would send Suzanne their profile and she would put it up on Pet Finder. Often times when my puppies arrived there were already potential adopters ready for them. Without Rescue Faerie I don't know how or where my puppies would have gone to get adopted. You can follow Rescue Faerie on IG @rescuefaerie or on FB The Rescue Faerie in Portland, Oregon.

Daniel Pena from Pelu Dogs. Daniel has always loved animals and he went to grooming school at Escuela de estetica canina professional Mr. Dog in 2005-2006 in Mexico City. He attended many grooming seminars and moved to Cabo in 2008. He then opened his first professional dog grooming salon in Cabo. Daniel is still very dedicated to pampering the dogs of Cabo and now has two locations opened. Daniel would groom for free all of my puppies that would travel by plane to their final destinations. He has also been my groomer since we got Vicente. My dogs love to have their spa day at Pelu Dogs. If you would like to know more about Pelu Dogs you can follow them @PeluDogs or FB Page Pelu Dogs on Cabo.

Mariana Perea Blazquez who owns and operates Dog Prana in Pescadero. Dog Prana was founded in 2011 and rescued puppies and found them homes in USA and Canada. They also started spay and neuter clinics for low-income families to get their animals fixed. Dog Prana also offers free workshops in schools to teach the children about the importance of caring for animals. Since Mariana was a small child, her goal was to rescue one dog at a time, give it a shower and haircut and return it back to its neighborhood. She wanted to be a zoologist or any field dealing with and working with animals. Even though Dog Prana is basically run by her and her daughter Ema, there are also many, many volunteers that help her out with fostering, rescuing, escorting the puppies to their final destinations and helping at the Dog Prana facility or at the spay and neuter clinics. Many of my puppies came from Dog Prana when she had too many puppies or wasn't able to take in puppies, then I would go and get them and foster them until they were ready to go to their 4ever homes. If you would like to know more about Dog Prana you can follow their Instagram Page @dogprana or FB page Dog Prana in Pescadero.

ABOUT THE AUTHOR

Penny Spade moved to Cabo San Lucas seventeen years ago and over the last fifteen years has fostered two hundred newborn puppies. These are some of her stories.

Made in United States
Troutdale, OR
08/04/2024

21755702R00062